Aniceti Kitereza
A Tanzanian Epic

Shoonie Hartwig

MKUKI NA NYOTA
DAR−ES−SALAAM

PUBLISHED BY
Mkuki na Nyota Pulishers Ltd
S. L. P. 4246
Dar es Salaam, Tanzania
www.mkukinanyota.com

ISBN 978-998-708-496-8

Visit www.mkukinanyota.com to read more about and to purchase any of Mkuki na Nyota books. You will also find featured authors interviews and news about other publisher/author events. Sign up for our e-newsletters for updates on new releases and other announcements. Distributed worldwide outside Africa by African Books Collective.

www.africanbookscollective.com

Contents

DEDICATION
For
Anna Katura
Aniceti Kitereza
Gerald Hartwig
And All Their Children

Acknowledgements

Without Jerry Hartwig's commitment to preserving historical documents, we would not have heard the voices of the many who tell this story of a story, in their own words.

From the beginning, Professor Joseph Mbele encouraged and edited this manuscript with a shared commitment to Kitereza's work.

Dr. Deborah Levinson's invitation for me to speak in her class at the University of Minnesota was the beginning.

Dr. David Sandgren wrote a review that has sustained me.

Walter Bgoya and Dr. Jamie Monson have faithfully walked Kitereza to the finish line.

Kristopher, Kari and Kurt. Since our Ukerewe days, you have faithfully followed in your dad's footsteps and by so doing, given me heart through these many years.

Kwa wote – Asanteni sana

Introduction

"Words that are spoken fly like the wind. Words that are written live forever."

Aniceti Kitereza spoke those words while telling Gerald (Jerry) and Charlotte (Shoonie) Hartwig the story of his novel. They were seated near Kitereza's mud and wattle home on the island of Ukerewe, in Tanzania. The year was 1969. They couldn't have imagined that this conversation would inaugurate an eleven-year saga, one of determination and commitment revealed in a significant collection of letters and the extraordinary tale of a man and a book.

The book you are holding is the story of this Tanzanian epic in words written and life lived. Aniceti Kitereza completed his epic novel in Kikerebe, his mother tongue, in early 1945 and later translated it as *Bwana Myombekere na Bibi Bugonoka na Ntulanalwo na Bulihwali*. Though translated into Swahili, French, German and English, this work is known to relatively few in Tanzania where his book might be read in select University global literature classes. The general public has yet to discover him; he remains remote and unknown.

What you will discover in these pages is not only the significant contribution of Kitereza's writing to African and world literature but also his heroic life as revealed through conversations and letters. It is his personal story captured particularly in the eighty blue aerograms written during his last years that bring his voice to life.

He was forty-nine years old when he completed *Myombekere* and eighty-one when his novel was published. His is an epic life to inspire not only Tanzanians but also the world, particularly as his life passion is encaptured in a question he posed: "What should we teach our children?"

For a proper appreciation of Kitereza, we should place him within an historical perspective in order to underline the fact that he is part of a long-standing tradition. The origin and evolution of this tradition is intimately tied up with the history of Africa itself: Africa, the cradle of the human race, and thereby of language and storytelling. Language as the principal means of self-expression and communication was also the principal vehicle of storytelling.

Since language originated and evolved as an oral phenomenon, storytelling or literature started as an oral tradition and remained such for millennia. For this reason, we do not have records of the earliest stories, songs and other forms of verbal art. However, the invention of writing made possible the textualization of oral literature and the creation of literature as a written tradition.

We do have evidence of these developments from ancient Egypt where the hieroglyphic script, created about five thousand years ago, was used to produce documents of various kinds, such as records of oral traditions and religious doctrines. Famous documents that have been deciphered include *The Egyptian Book of the Dead*, stories of deities such as Isis and Osiris, as well as folktales, such as "The Tale of Two Brothers" and "The Tale of the Shipwrecked Sailor." In fact, the oldest folktales we know are the ones written down by the ancient Egyptians.

There are other people in ancient Africa who developed writing traditions, such as the Libyans and the Ethiopians. The Ethiopians created the Ge'ez script that they used to record various traditions including religious teachings. Perhaps the best- known text in Ge'ez is *The Kebra Negast, The Book of Kings*, which recounts the tale of the early Queen of Ethiopia, her travel to King Solomon and how they got a child who became Emperor Menelik 1. Incorporating myths and legends as well, *The Kebra Negast* served to legitimize the rule of the royal family.

With the spread of Islam, the Arabic script was introduced in northern Africa, the Maghreb, the Sahel and the East African coast and adjacent islands. Writing in Arabic script evolved. In the Hausa and Swahili areas, the Arabic script was modified to suit the linguistic features of these languages and was used to write in various genres, such as historical chronicles and poetry.

With the coming of Europeans, literacy in European languages was introduced in Africa--mostly English, French and Portuguese. In the colonial schools and mission stations, Africans read European works of literature, some translated into African languages. A typical example was John Bunyan's *The Pilgrim's Progress*. These, together with translations of the Bible, fostered the kind of competence in written African languages that made it possible for a cadre of indigenous writers to emerge. That is how literature evolved in languages such as Xhosa, Zulu, Sotho, Shona, Yoruba and Kikuyu.

In East Africa, the immediate context for Kitereza, this pattern was replicated. The oldest written literary tradition in East Africa was in Swahili, with poetry being its mainstay from the beginning, in the seventeenth century. A classical tradition evolved, manifested in famous works such as the *Hamziya*, composed in the middle of the seventeenth century and based on an earlier Egyptian work, *Utendi wa Tambuka*, *Utendi wa Mwana Kupona*, and *Utenzi wa Rasi 'lGhuli*, all written before the coming of European rule.

Prose came later in the Swahili tradition, starting with travelogues, perhaps the best-known being that of Tippu Tip, which was part biography and part travelogue. This work of Tippu Tip's was published in several forms, including a German translation, between 1902 and 1905. It was published again, in 1966, as *Maisha ya Hamed bin Muhammed El Murjebi yaani Tippu Tip kwa Maneno Yake Mwenyewe*.

Like elsewhere in Africa, colonial and mission schools fostered literacy in East African languages such as Swahili, Ganda and Kikuyu, and with time, indigenous writers emerged in these languages. Under the tutelage of the Europeans, these writers tended to promote perspectives acceptable to their mentors. James Mbotela wrote *Uhuru wa Watumwa* which concerned the slave trade and the eventual rescue and rehabilitation of slaves by missionaries. It was the kind of vision presented earlier in Sesotho writer Thomas Mofolo's *Moeti wa Bochabela*.

However, there was also a deep commitment on the part of many of these early African writers to record African traditions, with the result that the creative writings of many of these writers appropriated traditional folklore. Classic examples are D. O.Fagunwa and Amos Tutuola in Yoruba, Gakaara wa Wanjau in Kikuyu and Thomas Mofolo in Sesotho.

If we take our cue from Kitereza and ask ourselves what we must teach our children, it seems necessary to pay attention to his particular historical background. It is necessary to acknowledge that he did not emerge and operate in a vacuum but that he inherited, participated in, and sought to preserve the age-old traditions and cultural heritage as they existed on Ukerewe.

It is appropriate to extend Kitereza's question beyond Ukerewe and argue that this understanding of the significance of Africa must occupy center stage in the education of our children. They must know that Africa was never the dark - continent it was alleged to be but shines forth as the origin of humanity. The same pride that Kitereza had for his people's culture ought to extend to the continent and beyond.

There is another way to look at Kitereza's ingenuity. Born under German colonialism, receiving his education in mission schools, he witnessed the encroachment of European culture on his society. He benefitted from the system by becoming conversant in several languages. Despite all this, however, he did not set out to glorify the influence of Europeans as did many African writers. Kitereza wanted to preserve the traditions of his people for all generations.

In this, he was driven by the same motives that impelled Elias Lonnrot of Finland to record the traditional songs of his people, which he synthesized and presented in the form of the Kalevala epic, so central to the identity of the Finnish people. A similar motive drove Chinua Achebe to write *Things Fall Apart* as a response to European writings about traditional Africa that he disliked because they did not present a truthful image.

As I have implied, other African writers writing within the European colonial and missionary environment appropriated European writings, such as *The Pilgrim's Progress* and Christian teachings. They judged African traditions as negative and looked to Europeans as agents of the Africans' redemption. Kitereza, remarkably, did not follow this trend. Though raised in the colonial and missionary environment, he sought to be the witness and the voice of the African traditions.

Although Kitereza's novel falls within the tradition of African written literature, it appropriates and is deeply rooted in Kikerebe oral tradition and folklore. He uses indigenous modes of storytelling and aesthetics. His novel, though a work of fiction, is a rich compendium of Kerebe customs. Kitereza stated categorically that he sought to preserve those customs for posterity, and it is remarkable that his work does not bear the imprint of its colonial and missionary context.

Indirectly, Kitereza's novel can be seen as an anti-colonial text in the sense that it refuses to acknowledge colonialism and instead celebrates the culture of the African people. In this way, his novel resembles Camara Laye's *The African Child*, which, in the midst of French colonialism in Guinea, focuses on celebrating traditional rural life.

Scholars of African literature dwell a great deal on the issue of writing in African languages, as well as the issue of translation of African language works. They talk about translating such works into not only

European and other foreign languages, but also into other African languages. Kitereza offers a unique point of reference on both counts. Those who advocate the translation of African language literatures into African languages can see Kitereza as a model; he wrote his novel in his mother tongue, Kikerebe, and then translated it into Swahili. To those who think about translating African literature into non-African languages, Kitereza offers a case study as well, since his novel has so far been translated into three European languages.

Within this book, *Aniceti Kitereza – A Tanzanian Epic,* Shoonie Hartwig tells the story of this epic man and his epic writing. When she and her husband Jerry lived on Ukerewe in 1968-69, their friendship with Kitereza became the catalyst for an eleven year saga of letter writing with one purpose: publish *Myombekere.*

There are two hundred and fourteen letters written. The correspondents are: Richard Markham, publisher at Heinemann in Nairobi, Kenya; John Allen, translator in Arusha, Tanzania; Jerry and Shoonie Hartwig in Durham, North Carolina; Emilie Larson, friend, in Boston, Massachusetts.

At the heart of these letter exchanges are Kitereza's eighty -seven blue aerograms written from Murutunguru, Ukerewe, Tanzania. This unique historic record gives us Kitereza's voice, as he meticulously writes, in his own words, about his life, about his wife, Anna, and about illness, and yet never giving in to despair. We hear Kitereza himself and we can only wonder at the magnificence of this man, as a husband, as a Tanzanian citizen, as an Mkerebe, as a Catholic, as a writer. In all these dimensions, he embodies the epic spirit.

Joseph L. Mbele
Associate Professor
English and Folklore
St. Olaf College
Minnesota, USA.

"What Must We Teach Our Children?"

One man's answer comes from a remote island in Lake Victoria where he realized that the wisdom of his people's folk tales, proverbs and music texts held life meaning guidance for future generations. The forces that gave him the passion to devote his life in pursuit of the answer are stories within a story, stories of how words spoken became words written, stories of inheritance teaching peaceful ways of living. Stories for everyone, everywhere.

It has been noted that there is only one Homer and there is only one Shakespeare for it was their classic epic writings that historically positioned Europe at the center of world literature. Now we must travel south from Greece and Great Britain to the continent of Africa and the country of Tanzania for it is there, on the island of Ukerewe in Lake Victoria, where we will discover that there is only one Kitereza.

Not only is his literary masterpiece, *Myombekere and Buganoka*, the longest written novel from the continent of Africa, the story of the author, Aniceti Kitereza, is epic in his heroic and courageous life of eight decades. From an obscure island in Lake Victoria comes a tale within a tale, a story of a man and his writing that places Tanzania at the heart of Africa's epic world.

During his life span from 1896 to 1981, Kitereza witnessed German and English rule, Catholic missionaries and traders whose presence threatened traditional ways of living. Trained in a Catholic seminary, he became a teacher, a clerk, a translator, an ethnographer, a collector of folk tales and proverbs, and finally a writer. At the center of Kitereza's writing is this question: "What must we teach our children?"

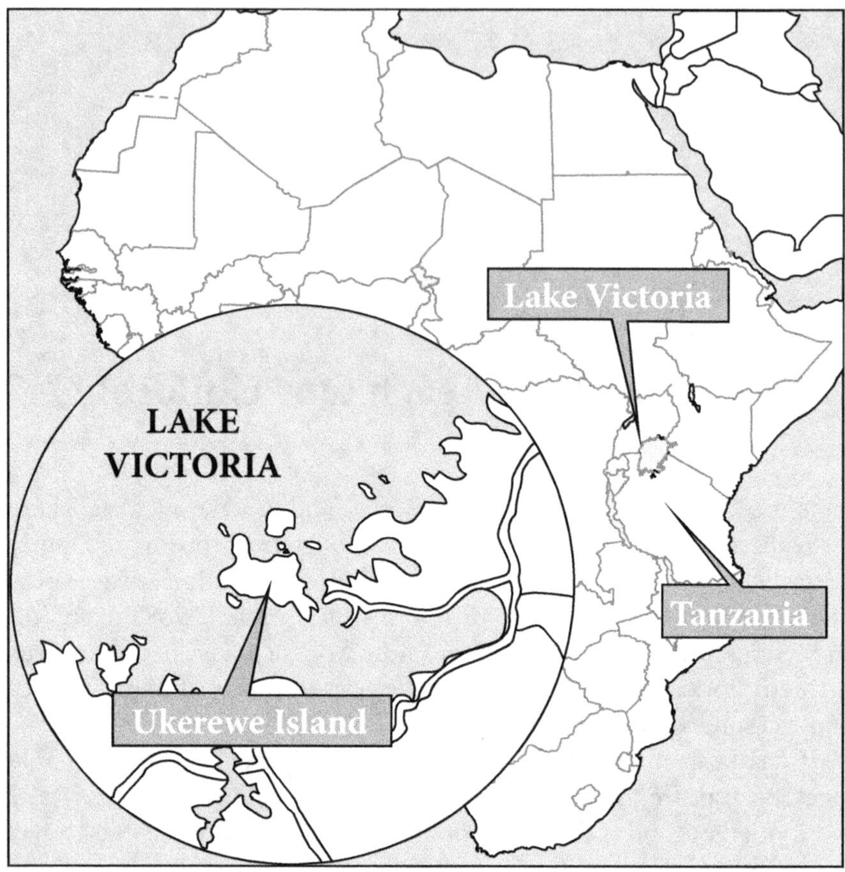

What is the source of this profound question? For a man who grew up only hearing stories, for a man who never owned a book other than a dictionary and a Bible, what caused him to write his own? What compelled him to write for children when none of his own lived beyond the age of four? This narrative of a living epic tells his story as well as his written answer to the question that is at the heart of his extraordinary ordinary life.

Kitereza's 'once upon a time' began in turmoil. 1896 was not a good year to be born. His father and mother had fled their island home on Ukerewe to the mainland of northeast Tanganyika seeking refuge from German power struggles. You may wonder how this could be. What could this remote island in Lake Victoria possibly have that a European power wanted?

Ukerewe's geographical position tells its own unique story. This once heavily timbered island is the largest in Lake Victoria with a land mass

MARA REGION
BUNDA
NAFUBA
UKARA
UKEREWE
UKEREWE DISTRICT
NANSIO
MWANZA
BWIRO
KISIRI
IRARA
NAMATEMBE
AABISHI
KIBITA
SIZU
CHIHARA
KIBINDA
MATUNBI
GALUSEILA
BURUN
IRERU
SIZA
GANA
LYAMBENGE
BUKIRU

seventy miles long and ten miles wide. Due to reliable rainfall, migrants from Tanganyika's mainland settled there assured of crop harvesting sufficient to ward off famine.

Kitereza's family was of the original Silanga/Sese ruling clan; his grandfather was the King or *Omukama*. The other migrant groups, the Jita, Sukuma and Kara, were subject to King Rukonge. They lived peacefully, farming beans and millet, herding cattle, hunting wild life on land and fishing or hunting hippos on the lake.

A year before Kitereza's birth, the Germans arrived on the island to claim it as their own. In Europe, as the industrial revolution took hold, the need for additional minerals and materials caused European leaders to look for other resource areas. The 'Scramble for Africa' meeting in Berlin in 1884 initiated the dividing of the continent with Tanganyika going to the Germans.

Ostensibly, the reason for European takeovers was to bring civilization to illiterate peasants whose barbaric ways would be replaced with western enlightenment.

Missionaries would save them through Christianity; schools would provide linguistic and educational tools to live well. And, the German's 'Anti-Slavery Society' would provide the moral banner for German takeover to be known as German East Africa.

The King soon realized that the German power structures could have a devastating impact on his people. It was more than the denial of his authority. The basic tenets of their society were challenged. The Bakerebe identity in language, in cultural values, in their ways of knowing how to live well was at risk of extinction.

Because of King Rukonge's resistance, the Germans deposed, exiled and jailed him. As a member of the royal family, Kitereza's mother and father fled with their new - born son to the mainland. However, within four years, his father died from smallpox. Kitereza and his mother then returned to Ukerewe to live within the King's compound.

As the German foothold became entrenched on Ukerewe soil, cotton and rice were introduced as cash crops and trees were felled for an increasing timber market. The Catholic Church joined the expatriate population in 1901 by sending French Canadian priests to establish schools as part of their mission outreach. For the majority of the Bakerebe, this was ignored with a strong show of resistance.

However, within the royal household, an interest in how these foreigners gained power had been ignited. Kitereza was sent to school to discover their secrets.

At the age of nine, Kitereza began his own educational journey, one that would weave between the formal and the informal, between classroom study and evening firelight storytelling. An apt pupil, the Catholic priests suggested that he enter the seminary, a worthy candidate for the priesthood.

Kitereza was thirteen years old.

He spent ten years at Rubya Seminary, located on the mainland mastering Latin, the language of Roman Catholic institutions. He learned Greek, a requirement of the seminary and German, the language of the colonizers. He already knew Kiswahili, the African language of traders and merchants, while already proficient in Kikerebe, the language of his clan.

More changes were ahead with the defeat of the Germans in World War I. As a result, German East Africa was divided into Ruanda-Urundi and given to the Belgians while Tanganyika went to the British as a League of Nations mandate, and at the end of World War II in 1946, it became a United Nations Trust Territory still under British rule. Kitereza then learned English.

By now, he was a young adult male. Becoming a priest meant celibacy; it meant giving up one of the primary identity markers of being Kerebe – having children. He had already changed his first name to Aniceti, a requirement upon conversion to Catholicism. But not to marry? He decided to leave the seminary and soon after, he married Anna Kutura.

Kitereza was twenty-three years old.

Given Kitereza's educational background, he found employment first with the Mwanza Rice Mill as a clerk and purchaser and then with the East African Rice Mills. However, with the outbreak of World War II, normal economic development ceased causing Kitereza and Anna to return to the Kagunguli mission on the island.

It was here that his writing genesis began. He was assigned to work with a French Canadian priest, Father J. A. Simard, as a translator of religious materials. Father Simard recognized Kitereza's keen intellect. He encouraged him to begin collecting undocumented legacies of his own people, thus initiating a creative ethnographic and writing life to sustain him all his days.

As Kitereza's documenting of folk tales, music texts and proverbs grew to a significant collection, he became acutely aware of this treasure from his own people. He had lived through the changes on Ukerewe brought by outsiders. He had witnessed the erosion of his peoples' values. Within this ethnographic process came a new realization. If he didn't write about these cultural ways of the past, the Bakerebe inheritance would be lost. Kitereza's question - "What must we teach our children?" – became the heart of his epic saga.

A folk tale from Kitereza's collection that illustrates this well is a story about a white-faced monkey and a black-faced lizard who want to be friends. Their dilemma is not only differences in their physical appearance but in their cultural norms. The leader or king of each group declares that they must 'become like one of us' before friendship is possible.

On an island where, at first glance, everyone seems related, difference is profoundly hidden in language and marriage customs for starters. As you will read, there is no direct answer to Kitereza's question as to what we should teach our children. However, the tale of *Enkwambu and Enkende* raises the profound question of what is required if differences are to be overcome so that we might live together, peacefully. This dilemma tale's English adaptation lends itself well to theater mime as well as other forms of performance.

Enkwambu and Enkende

I have a little story that I think you will like

About a monkey who is black and a lizard who is white
Enkwambu, the monkey, was walking one day
When he met Enkende, the lizard, so he stopped to say
"Listen, my friend, come to my house and eat – I promise I'll
fix you a very special treat!"

With delight the lizard asked, "When will this be"
And Enkwambu, the monkey, said –"Tomorrow, I'm free."
The monkey hurried home to tell his wife
Cause they'd never fed a lizard in their entire life!

The monkey said, "Lizards like intestines of a fish."
His wife said, "You really think that's a tasty dish?"
The monkey said, "I'm off to see our chief, for I'm sure he'll
agree To make our friend the lizard part of our family!"
When the lizard arrived the next day to dine, Everything was
prepared especially fine
The chair, the table, everything was set

If only the chief's rules could be easily met.

The monkey said, "Friend, I'm sure you'll agree— Good
friends are just part of one big family!
My chief said you can become one of us

If you'll seat in a chair, without too much fuss!"

So the lizard tried – and he tried – and he tried some more
But he ALWAYS landed – on the floor.
Sadly, the lizard went home.

Later that week, the monkey was walking one day
And he met the lizard, who stopped to say –
"Listen, my friend, come to MY house and eat – I promise I'll
fix you a very special treat!"
With delight the monkey asked, "When will this be?"
Enkende, the lizard, said, "Tomorrow, I'm free!"
The lizard hurried home to tell HIS wife,

Cause they'd NEVER fed a monkey in their entire life! The
lizard said, "Monkeys think corn is good food!"
His wife said, "If I told you what I think, you'd say that I'm
rude!"
The lizard said, "I'm off to see our chief, for I'm sure he'll
agree
To make our friend the monkey part of our family."
When the monkey arrived the next day to dine,
Everything was prepared especially fine.
The chair, the table, everything was set

If only the chief's rules could be easily met. The monkey sat
happily, ready to eat
The corn prepared especially as a tasty treat.
The lizard said, "Friend, I'm sure you'll agree –
Good friends are just part of one big family! My chief said
you can become one of us –
Just make your face white – like MINE – without too much
fuss!"

So the monkey washed, and he washed, and he scrubbed his
face sore. But alas, he was just as black as before.
Now my friends, it is obvious to see
That God's been very busy, creating you and me!
The question is – DO we belong – to one big family?

Kerebe Folk Tale

As Kitereza began to write, his approach was dry and academic for
that was what he knew from the seminary. His collection was of value
to new European priests assigned to the island but hardly suitable for
children. Father Simard suggested that Kitereza write a story, for then
children would be interested.

In 1945, Kitereza completed his novel written in two parts. The first,
Bwana Myombekere na Bibi Bugonoka tells of Myombekere and his wife,
Bugonoka who are unable to have children. This cultural curse is cause
for Myombekere to seek another wife. How they, as a couple, resist
family pressures to remain together is their story weaving themes of
curses and blessings, men and women, health and illness, war and peace.
The second part, *Ntulanalwo na Bulihwali*, Myombekere and Bugonoka's

children, continues the tale as their family struggles with the central survival issues of production and reproduction.

The story so impressed Father Simard that he had it typed – all three hundred fifty typewritten, single-spaced pages. Father Simard approached a publisher in East Africa so that it could be used in primary schools. But this was in the early 1950s and, given the limited readership of Kikerebe, Kitereza's manuscript was rejected.

Kitereza was forty-nine years old.

During the ensuing years, Kitereza's name became familiar to islanders and also to outside researchers as a rare ethnographer, a collector of oral traditions. As interested people came to his door promising publication, two of the typewritten copies vanished. By 1968, only one copy remained. Father Van Der Wee, who continued to mentor Kitereza following Fr Simard's death, placed the final copy under lock and key in the seminary on the mainland.

Kitereza was seventy-two years old.

A Translation Epic

A doctoral student in African Studies at Indiana University had read about Ukerewe's unusual oral traditions connected to long distance trade. In 1968, African Studies was a newly admitted focus of study in higher education. Although significant research had been written, the gap of knowledge between documented history and oral tradition was significant. This gap intrigued the researcher.

His dissertation would explore how critical oral traditions were to the interpretation of researched historical events. Jerry Hartwig was not a newcomer to Tanzania as he had taught at Ilboru secondary school near Arusha from 1961 to 1964. With his wife, Shoonie and three children, Kristopher, Karl and Kari, the Hartwig family had already learned other ways of knowing and being. They were eager to discover more on Ukerewe.

Arriving on the island in the spring of 1968, Kitereza's name was one of the first given as a key informant. Hartwig's first visits were part of a process that became very familiar with all his informants. No Kerebe would volunteer any information to an outsider – and certainly not to a white man – without first knowing who he was, where he came from, what he was doing and why.

It took several weeks to develop trust, weeks of repeated visits with *chai* and *ugali* punctuating conversations. And then came the invitation from Kitereza for Hartwig to bring his family. It isn't enough to know a man and what he does, his family is his lifeblood, his future, his most valued possession. It was natural then, that Kitereza's warm hospitality would be extended to include all in the Hartwig family.

As they approached Kitereza's home, they called, *"Hodi, hodi,"* anyone home?" as is the custom to announce one's arrival. From inside his mud and wattle home, a deep, resonant voice responded, *"Karibu, karibu!"* In a few moments, Kitereza stood framed in the doorway, an aging man of medium build, his balding head circled with a fringe of grey. Clad in a red, turtleneck sweater and khaki pants, he slowly emerged with the help of a walking stick.

It was hard to ignore his swollen and misshapen hands and feet, for walking was clearly painful. Yet one look at this man's face and his physical difficulties were forgotten. Warmth, friendliness and patience creased his smile of welcome as he welcomed each of us with a firm handshake.

An aura of dignity permeated this clean-swept courtyard shaded by mango and lemon trees as he eased himself into a chair near his wife, Anna,. It almost seemed as if Kitereza were holding court. The now-erect posture as he viewed his guests made it obvious that this was a man who knew where he came from and that he took great pride in his origins.

Anna, his wife, said little. A small, frail woman, she quietly added smiles and nods to the conversation but she seldom spoke. This was the woman who had been Kitereza's only wife, the woman who had borne four children and had suffered as each of them died before they reached age four. Kitereza had left schooling and seminary to marry her. Anna had left her family on the Tanzanian mainland one hundred miles away to marry him.

Unlike the other compounds where many houses are close together so that parents, grandparents and children intermingle constantly in all their daily activities, Anna and Kitereza's house stood alone. There was no chatter of voices around them; their humble, thatched-roof home stood isolated. In their old age, they were experiencing unspeakable loneliness. With no children to care for them, they were completely dependent upon one another.

Together, as far as they were able, they cultivated their rice, cassava and beans. They grew what their energies allowed them to plant but Anna suffered from a heart condition, sapping her energy and limiting her activity. Their food came from what they could grow. If the rains were good, they could eke out enough to survive but it was day- to-day survival. In spite of Kitereza's education and his many abilities, his life showed no evidence of any financial rewards.

As the conversation turned to Kitereza's writing, his expression darkened as clouds before a storm. Scorn and disappointment accented Kitereza's voice as he began to relate the sad story of his novel and in particular the ethnographers seeking him out, promising publication as they took his manuscript.

"I now have a new proverb," he said. "When the Europeans came, they treated us like monkeys and took everything from us that they wanted." But then, as Kitereza began to talk about the novel itself, the sun began to shine. As he described the characters, the theme of the story and how he used Kerebe folk tales and proverbs, Anna said nothing. Yet, her face reflected all the love and affection in Kitereza's voice.

His words suddenly ceased to be mere sentences. It was poetic speech full of an almost parental concern and hope. For twenty-three years, they had waited to see his cherished words in print. For twenty-three years, they had the faith and hope that each tomorrow might bring the book to publication.

When Hartwig asked Kitereza to tell us about his writing, this is what he said:

> I finished writing this book on February 13, 1945, a book I wrote out of my deeply felt desire to preserve the Customs and Way of Life of our Ancestors, Fearing this great way of life of our ancestors and the principles that governed them would one day disappear and be completely forgotten, I felt I had to write them down, otherwise future generations of our people would lose their rightful Heritage of the customs and traditions of their ancestors. The prospect of such a loss filled me with great pity for the generations of our people to come, and so I looked for the best way of telling them how their ancestors lived.

> That's why I decided to write this story…It was obvious to me that writing this book in a story would make people want to read the book more. But above all, I wanted this to be a way of preserving the language of our ancestors, by showing the reader how beautifully they spoke to each other, whether it was in their neighborly conversations during palavers in each others' homes or simply in the casual exchange of greetings between even total strangers who chanced to meet on the roads, who too would always politely exchange with each other greetings and news of wherever they were coming from and inform each other of where they were going."

> This country would be lost for our children and the children not yet born if they were not written down, for how else will they be preserved? I selected a method: it would be best to put these words in a book. I wrote in Kikerebe so that the customs of our fathers would be known in this place of Bukerebe.

> And so concerning these matters, I began carefully to search for those secrets of long ago, those things loved and those things despised. After I began to more fully understand, I realized that the most despised person was one unable to have children, whether a man or a woman. Such a man – mgumba –was greatly ridiculed by those whose fortune was good, those who were able to bear children.

> There is not a man who is able to say 'As for me, I'd not have death in my body!' If he does, he is a fool.' Can life have meaning without children? One day a man may have wealth, strength in body and joy in heart, but tomorrow, it may all vanish leaving grief beyond measure. Misfortune comes with no warning. It can occur in the morning. At any time. These things are the power of God. To hide a disease is to want it revealed by mourners.

When Kitereza spoke these words, he had been waiting twenty-two years for his novel to be published. The tale of his waiting is an epic within an epic.

A Publishing Epic

When the Hartwigs left Kitereza and Anna after that first meeting, they knew that they had been in the presence of an extraordinary man. Before saying their '*kwa heri's*', two promises were made. First, Hartwig would take the ferry to Mwanza on the mainland to secure the one remaining copy of Kitereza's manuscript kept at the Catholic mission. Second, he would seek possible publishers.

Not unlike any road trip in Tanzania, this extraordinary publishing safari would be fraught with potholes, diversions and tire blowouts. Perseverance and good faith would be required over what at times seemed an endless journey of eleven years.

Once the one remaining copy was secured from the Catholic mission in Mwanza, copies of the first section were sent to the Institute of Kiswahili in Dar es Salaam. Their response was immediate: the readership of Kikerebe was too small to warrant publishing. Before further consideration, he would need to translate his book from Kikerebe to Kiswahili.

Kitereza set up his office under the shade of their mango tree with two orange crates for his desk to begin the laborious task of meticulously translating the first chapters.

It was now early June. Nearing the end of the rainy season, damp cold meant necessary retreats into their humble home bereft of good light and too many roof leaks. His gnarled fingers and swollen hands would have sufficed as a deterrent to this gargantuan task. Not Kitereza.

Kitereza was seventy-three years old.

Over the next eight months, the Hartwig family made frequent visits to Kitereza's compound bringing tablets and pens to keep the translating author well supplied. On one occasion, they brought a visiting friend from Boston, Massachusetts, a meeting that would be life changing for Emilie Larson and for Aniceti.

This middle-aged spinster, this Bostonian proper woman, met the Hartwigs during their Harvard days as they attended the same Lutheran church. She often wore white gloves, was always modest in attire and always striding around in sturdy shoes. A prim and proper middle-aged woman, her bent forward posture encompassed a woman with a passion for student learning. As a junior high counselor, her devotion to them was clear, but Boston under-stated.

When Emilie learned of the Hartwig's research time on Ukerewe, she asked if she might visit, along with her nephew, David. Of all the possible visitors, she was not on their list. They simply couldn't imagine how she would manage the daunting Arusha– Mwanza road trip to say nothing of island living. Their concerns were for naught.

Before the Kitereza visit, she listened attentively to the details of his life, his writing and the Hartwigs' commitment to publish his book. But first, he needed to translate the Kikerebe text to Kiswahili before it could be considered for publication.

Emilie was well acquainted with those who publish. Growing up in the barren, flat farm -lands of North Dakota, her three aunts were sent to Boston's Radcliff College in the early 1900's. Subsequently, each earned her doctorate, each published significantly in chemistry, economics and history. Emilie was embarked upon her own writing project focused on middle school learners.

When Larson and Kitereza met, it was a meeting of kindred spirits. Emilie not only had suggestions but she acted on them. Might the journal of *Natural History* be interested in an article? She would make the initial contacts. And what of Kitereza's continuing need for papers, pens and postage? How might she assist? Might Ben- Gay ointment help his increasing rheumatic pain?

After a three -week stay on Ukerewe, Emilie returned to Boston, to middle school student counseling and pursuit of a *Natural History* commitment. She also initiated a monthly ten- dollar check to support Kitereza as well as ointments for his rheumatism.

When the Hartwigs returned to graduate school in Bloomington, Indiana, Jerry hand-carried his dissertation notes and Shoonie hand-carried Kitereza's first chapter translations.

A Kerebe Tale

How Men and Women Came to Live Together

by Aniceti Kitereza

Now listen and I will tell you an old story so that you may know what made us live with women. In the beginning, all men lived together in one country with their Chief. They cultivated grain that they used as food, but they never ate meat. At this same time, women lived in another country with their Queen. The women did not know how to cultivate grain, so they ate only meat. The Queen had trained one hundred dogs that would help her women catch wild animals for their meat supply.

One day the Queen sent for her Headwoman and her messengers and said: "Go to the men's country to greet their Chief. See if those people are peaceful and bring me news from them."

said the men, "for it is taboo for us. How do you manage to capture the wild animals?"

"Our Queen has trained one hundred dogs. These dogs are very clever, and they catch the wild animals for us."

Now this was pleasant news to the Chief for he was constantly harassed by wildlife that destroyed his crops. Suddenly he had an idea.

"Could your Queen lend me her dogs so that we might be rid of these pests who rob us of our food and ruin our grain?"

"Surely, she will gladly do so."

"How many dogs do you think she could spare?" the Chief inquired.

"Perhaps she will lend you all of them, but of course, we cannot an-

rageous custom. Eager for details, they asked for more information concerning this strange food.

One of the Queen's messengers began to explain: "There are some rootlike plants that are round in shape. They are called *enumbu*, 'sweet potatoes.' And there are other plants like trees called *amalibwa*, 'cassava, or manioc.' There are also some grasslike plants and when they have been dried and harvested, the grains are separated from the stalks. This pure grain is called *oburo*, 'millet.' It can be stored in a special house until the men need it. Then it is put on a grinding stone and ground into flour. Water is boiled and the flour is added until it is very stiff and the large wooden ladle cannot

Emilie's query letter to *Natural History* bore fruit. The Hartwigs submitted an article that included an excerpt from Kitereza's novel, *How Men and Women Came to Live Together*. It was published in 1970. Because *Natural History* pays contributors by the column, Kitereza received sufficient funds to replace his leaking thatch roof with rain-resistant bati.

That same year, in the journal *Research in African Literature,* the Hartwigs published an article focused on Kitereza. With this quick publishing response giving initial exposure to Kitereza's writing, hopes for successful publishing in Tanzania seemed probable.

In October 1970, the Institute of Kiswahili Research in Dar es Salaam received the first translated chapter. Their response was devastating. Kitereza's Swahili was old fashioned; it did not comply with their guidelines, therefore, they could not consider it for publication.

This refusal, daunting as it was, did not deter Jerry Hartwig. The next contact would be to Heinemann's in Nairobi. Their head office in London and East African office in Kenya launched The African Writer's Series in 1962. The names of Achebe, Kaunda, Samkange and others became known, first in African universities and schools and gradually, in the U.S. These writers wrote in English; their novels intentionally addressed post- colonial themes. Kitereza didn't fit the established mode, but might they consider his significant contribution to African literature?

Hartwig sent the first pages of Kitereza's translation with an introductory background to Markham, Heinemann's senior editor. He, in turn, sent it on to their Kiswahili editor, John Allen, living in Arusha, Tanzania. Allen's response was so positive, he envisioned this novel to be a unique contribution to African literature. How soon could the author provide a translation of all 350 pages?

Under the mango tree in his compound on Ukerewe, in the village of Murutunguru, Kitereza laboriously continued to translate his entire novel into Kiswahili. The promise that his words, first spoken, would be written as a legacy for the next generation moved his gnarled hands to write.

No one could have imagined how long it would take before Kitereza's words would be birthed to live in print. Nor could anyone have anticipated the many key people who would communicate through letters with one goal in mind: Publish Kitereza's book.

This significant collection of letters is an epic publishing story. Until these letters began, Kitereza had never written on a blue aerogram,

page 1.

KIPINDI CHA KWANZA.

Bwana MYOMBEKERE na BI. BUGONOKA.

SURA YA KWANZA.

Bw. Myombekere ananyang'anywa mke wake Bugonoka.

Myombekere na Bugonoka walioana baada ya kutimiza haja zote za desturi na sheria za ndoa, walipokuwa bado wote vijana. Ulipita mwaka moja mzima; na katika mwaka wa pili uliyofuata, Bugonoka akawa mja mzito. Mimba hiyo ilidumu muda wa miezi nne; na katika mwezi wa tano mimba ikaharibu, mtoto wa kiume! — Baada ya siku chache, mwanamke akaingia miezini na akapata tena mimba ya pili; na hiyo ilidumu nayo kwa muda wa miezi sita, tena katika mwezi wa saba vilevile mimba ikaharibu akatoka mtoto wa kike; kitoto kiliishi siku moja tu siku ya pili yake kikaaga dunia! — Basi tangu hapo mwanamke wa Myombekere hakuzidi tena kuwa mimba, walikaa muda wa myaka mingi wakiwa Wagumba.

Hapo jamaa wa Myombekere wakaanza kuwaka hasira na kupayuka wakimwambia akatae mke wake, wakisema: "Wewe ni ndugu yetu, sasa unakubali kweli kukaa na mke wako huyu akiwa mgumba hivi, uzuri wako huu wote uishie chini!! — Sasa wewe unadhani kufefuka kwa watu hapa duniani ni nini? — Si kuzaa na kuacha mbegu yako ikiwa hai, hiyo ndiyo maendeleo ya ukoo wetu; Kama wewe baba yako na mama yako hawangekuzaa, ungetoka wapi? — Kisha mwanaume yeyote hawi (mgumba) hanywi dawa kamwe: Dawa ya mwanaume ni kuushika upindi na kwenda kuposa. Na wewe ukiposa, ukaoa kwa umri wako uliyo nao huwezi kukosa kuzaa!"

Yeye Myombekere akawajibu akasema: "Sasa nyinyi mwataka nifanye nini?"

Jamaa zake wakanena: "Sisi tunataka umkatae mke wako huyu, uoe mungine, ukae; sababu kama ukikaa na huyu tu, hutafanikiwa kupata mtoto kamwe!"

never exchanged letters with anyone outside of the Kerebe world. These are the primary correspondents:

Aniceti Kitereza – Murutunguru, Ukerewe Tanzania

Jerry Hartwig – Duke University – Durham, N.C.
R. Markham – Heinemanns – Nairobi, Kenya,
John Allen – translator – Arusha, Tanzania Emilie Larson - Boston, MA.
Catholic Fathers – Murutunguru, Ukerewe

Their letters span the eleven years between 1969 and 1980 during which two hundred and fourteen letters were written. Eighty -seven are Kitereza's aerograms translated from Swahili to English. This extraordinary epistolary epic captures the spirit, the space and the heart of all contributors.

1969

This first year shows how the relationship between Kitereza, Catholic Fathers and Larson is focused on health remedies for rheumatism and publishing an excerpt from his book in the journal of *Natural History*. The Hartwigs are still present on Ukerewe.

February 8, 1969 Larson to Kitereza

Dear Mr. Kitereza: I thank you for your beautiful letter. Indeed, I shall never forget our hour with you in the afternoon sun, talking of many things. David and I recall our three days on Ukerewe as a high point of our lives.

I cannot tell you how pleased I am that you are translating your book into Swahili. What you are writing about Ukerewe will be lost forever unless you put it down. To put thoughts on paper is very hard work. It is so wonderful that you translate it yourself so that you retain the meaning of the words and thought and poetry of the language.

I have sent more money to the Hartwigs for you and I shall send medicine with directions so they read directions to you. There are not many medicines for rheumatism. I will do my best. To keep warm and dry is very important.

Writing is laborious – the hardest work I do. But do not give up hope. If the warm sun has come, you may feel better, and what you have is important. Sincerely, Emilie Larson

MARCH 8, 1969, LARSON TO EDITORIAL OFFICE - MUSEUM OF NATURAL HISTORY

Gentlemen: In about a month I shall receive the manuscript of a short story from Mr. Kitereza of Ukerewe Island, Lake Victoria, Tanzania. The story is entitled, "How Men and Women Came to Live Together". I realize that no one will make a judgment of a manuscript until he has read it. I am wondering if a member of your organization would be willing to read the manuscript so as to advise me what its prospects might be?... Sincerely, Miss Emilie Larson.

JULY 15, 1969   KITEREZA TO LARSON (ENGLISH TRANSLATION, FATHER MATTE)

Miss Emilie Larson, Thank you very much for your letter of June 26, which I received on July 9, 1969. I am also very thankful for your marvelous gift of $10 dollars, the equivalent of 70/shillings. I am also very grateful for the saving medication that you sent to me.

When I opened your letter I was terribly thrilled and highly excited longing to hear what you were going to say. My wife was also very anxious to hear what you had written. Thank you ever so much for having remembered me at my moment of need. I pray God to preserve you for many more years to come. God's blessings be upon you.

I guess you do realize the extent of our poverty which recently was made even worse by hurricane force winds that tore away a part of my hut. My rheumatism has handicapped me so badly that I find it extremely difficult to repair my house. I cannot go into the woods and chop wood for the needed repairs and my wife is too weak to be of any significant help. At this moment I am looking toward you to help me to reinforce my meager resources, so that I can hopefully afford to buy about 20 corrugated sheets to rebuild my shattered shack. That's the sad news from me.

When I received your check, I went to see an Indian in Nansio who helped me to exchange the dollars for shillings. However, he demanded 10% of the check for the price of the transaction. So I ended up having only 57 shillings instead of 70. The Canadian priest who used to help me cash the checks has been transferred to another parish so I have no other alternative. Give my best wishes to David and his sister.

Aniceti Kitereza

The following letter acknowledges receipt of monies that Hartwig forwarded to Aniceti to the amount of $100. *Natural History* had responded positively, agreeing to publish, "How Men and Women Came to Live Together". The advance of the promised payment was sent to a new parish priest. The Hartwigs are now back in the States.

OCTOBER 19, 1969 FATHER DESCHAMPS-UKEREWE TO HARTWIG

Dear Mr. Hartwig. We received your letter Friday; I went to see Aniceti yesterday and gave him 650 shillings and I will give him the exact balance when I receive the statement from the bank. So everything is settled for the moment.

Aniceti is very happy about the business. He seems to understand the whole matter well. This windfall is certainly a blessing for him; his house badly needs a roof and soon. His health is not so good; he can hardly walk because of his rheumatism.

Greetings to your wife. Best regards from Father Karel and others here. Sincerely, R. Deschamps W.F.

1970

The letter exchanges begin to expand as the quest for a publisher continues. R. C. Markham at Heinemanns in Nairobi becomes a faithful contributor to this saga.

---

9 February 1970 Kitereza to Hartwigs

I received the letter you sent me a month ago. I was sad to read that Christopher, Charel and Kari have been ill. These days, I have also been sick with dysentery and it has left me with no strength in my body.

Miss Emilie Larson sent me a picture from Natural History. I was very happy to see my words in print. There is a picture of Bwana and Mama Hartwig. But underneath your picture it says: Charlotte Hartwig. WHO IS THIS? (Charlotte is her legal name and not known to Kitereza.) *My picture with me seated at my poor table made me very happy and when I called Anna Katura, she, too, was very excited. You have written about my life, Mr. G. J. Hartwig, and it is well done... A.K.*

---

13 April 1970 Kitereza to Hartwigs

Dear Bwana and Mama of Hartwig children. How are all of you these many days since you left the island of Ukerewe. From your letter, I know you work very hard – Mama typing history notes and my translations and caring for the children. I hope they are all well...I am waiting for the promised monies to help me in my shamba. I send greetings to all of you. May God give you a long life! My wife, Anna Katura sends you special greetings for Easter. Greetings from your friend, Mzee Aniceti Kitereza

24 SEPTEMBER 1970 KITEREZA TO HARTWIG

Dear Jerry! You have asked me how I am doing with the writing/ translation. I have had health problems, first with diarrhea for some time. Also, because of my rheumatism, if I sit at my desk for even a short time, my legs begin to swell. But I try as much as I can to continue the translation. Thank you for the monies sent! Anna Katura, my wife, sends her greetings. We are happy that Mrs. Shoonie birthed a son. Kurt is what sex? May God be with all of you. Yours, A.K

27 OCTOBER 1970 HARTWIG TO HEINEMANN'S - LONDON COPY TO KITEREZA

Dear Sirs:

During 1968 and 1969, I collected historical traditions among the Kerebe (kerewe) of Tanzania, a people inhabiting a large island in the southeastern portion of Lake Victoria. It was during this time that I met Aniceti Kitereza, the subject of this letter.

Mr. Kitereza is now 74 years of age and received his formal education between 1905 and 1918 under the direction of the Roman Catholic White Fathers. Employed briefly as a teacher following World War I, he subsequently found employment as a clerk for an Italian businessman until the outbreak of war in 1939 when his employer was repatriated. During the war years he worked as a clerk for a Canadian White Father. At this time he assisted the priest in assembling ethnographic data, compiling a dictionary, etc. Emanating from this work was a project designed to incorporate the ethnographic material into a format that would be interesting to pupils in the local primary schools Consequently Mr. Kitereza wrote a story of a young married couple who experienced difficulty in conceiving a child. One of his motives for writing this type of story was to teach the children about their community's former customs, already irrevocably altered by the 1940s.

The story or novel was to have been published in Kikerebe by the East African Literature Bureau but the project was apparently economically unsound since the number of potential readers was limited. The priest who encouraged Mr. Kitereza died in the early 1950s and the typed manuscript has been in 'storage' for some two decades. My wife and I extracted a tale from the novel and published it earlier this year; a copy is enclosed for your perusal.

After discussing the possibilities of publishing his work with him, it was agreed that Mr. Kitereza would translate the original manuscript into

Aniceti Kitereza
P.O.B 16 Nansio, Ukerewe Island
c/o Kagunguli Parish
Date 7 Jan. 1971. Tanzania Africa.

Bwana G.W. Hartwig!

Barua yako tukufu ya 21 December 1970, nimeipokea 29 Dec. 1970. Nilipoisoma tu nikaona kwamba umenitumia Copy ya Barua uliyomwandikia Mr. R.C. Markham wa Nairobi, Kenya.

Nimefahamu yakama tarehe ileile ya 21 December 1970, ndiyo umempelekea Maandiko ya mkono ya Kiswahili, yaani ya Kitabu changu. — Na kwamba unatumainia kupata majibu kwa wakati ujao.

Ninakusifu sana Bwana Hartwig, kwa matendo yako ya uhodari wa kutia bidii sana, juu ya kusaidia na kutafuta Wapigaji chapa wa Vitabu; kwani kazi hiyo ___ ni ngumu kabisa!

Mimi ninakusihi Sana Jerry, kama Kitabu chetu hicho, kingechapishwa kwa lugha mbili, yaani; lugha ya Kiingereza, na Vitabu vingine katika lugha ya Kiswahili. — Mimi tena kwa mawazo yangu, ningependa sana Kitabu kile kitiwe Picha (Illustration) ndani yake, katika kila sura (chapter), kwa sababu ya mazungumzo matamu ya watu waliomo! — Hapo ingekuwa kama sinema (cinema) nzuri sana ya kupendeza watu. — Kwa sababu mimi hapa, watu huwa wanafika hapa kwangu na kuuliza za: "Je, namna gani, Kitabu chako Myombekere na Bugonoka, kimekawisha kucha pishwa?" Mimi ninawajibu kila mara hivi: "Bado!" — Na wao huniulaumu yakama mimi nimekuwa mjinga sitaweza kupata chochote juu ya Kitabu chako, kwa maana kimekwenda mbali!! — Tumefurahi mwa na miye kututolea Salaam za Kristmas ya 1970! — Tunawapeni pole ya mwaka 1971! — Nimefahamu kwamba shughuli za shule zimepungika, kwa hiyo utakuyo majuma 2 ya kujipatia kazi yako. Tena nimeelewa Wazazi wako wanakuja kuwaam kia na kustinda nanyi muda wa siku 16, tena mna tagania kwa furaha na kustarehe Familia yenu kujiti kuungana pamoja! — Eh! mliifurahi sana kweli ya moja na Wazee wako!

Kimeelewa kwamba unatumainia kusikia jambo mojawapo kutoka kwa Mr. R.C. Markham katika mwezi wa March au April.

Habari juu ya Synopsis, karibu nitakwisha kilichonipa kuchelewa Bwana Jerry, ni sababu

Kiswahili after which I would then submit it to a publisher. Beginning in December 1968, he laboriously commenced this translation task which he completed by March 1970, some fifteen months later.

The original manuscript was a typed, single-spaced 300 page work; the Kiswahili version, now in my possession, fills over 850 legal-sized pages in long hand. It has now been duplicated and is ready for assessment. Mr. Kitereza's Kiswahili is regarded as being dated; however, the manuscript as it now reads has the advantage of being translated by the author and he is extremely sensitive to the nuances of language having learned Latin, German, French and English in addition to Kiswahili.

If you would be interested in looking at the manuscript, I would gladly forward a copy to you. I have been informed that Heinemann's is now publishing some works in Kiswahili. But if the manuscript possesses the merits I think it contains, an English translation should be considered.

The rationale for his writing the novel in the first instance attracted my attention: its readership was envisaged as the young people of his own community. This poses problems of its own but I feel the advantages of such a work far exceed the disadvantages. Sincerely, Gerald W. Hartwig cc. Aniceti Kitereza

---

15 November 1970 Kitereza to Hartwig Bwana Jerry!

I am so happy to have received two letters from you. The first, dated 1 October 1970 arrived the 23rd of October. I read that your children are all in school – Kristopher in sixth grade, Karl in fourth and Kari in 2nd. Loo! Really, their mama taught them well before going back to school. And you have finished writing, "A Cultural History of the Kerebe of Tanzania Before 1895". Now you will receive your degree.

You also asked me to write a 'synopsis' of my book. I've asked before and I ask again, Bwana Jerry, please send me an example so that I can write it well. Maybe you forgot to send me an example because you are so busy, but if you send me the example, I will write it. So I wait here for your answer.

Padre Deschamps of Murutunguru brought me two more writing books and bic pens. From 1 October to the 26th, I was in the hospital. My wife was with me. My rheumatism continues to bother me greatly with swelling in my legs. These days I am cold from morning to night. Miss Emilie Larson sent money to help at the hospital.

Greet Mama watoto Shoonie and your family. Aniceti Kitereza

24 November 1970 James Curry/Heinemanns-London to Hartwig

Dear Dr. Hartwig,

Thank you for your letter of 27 October 1970. We are, indeed, publishing books in Kiswahili. We should certainly be most interested to consider this manuscript, even though it sounds very long. I suggest that you send it directly to:

> *Mr. R. Markham, Managing Director Heinemann Educational East Africa*
> *P. O. Box 25080 Nairobi, Kenya*

This really does sound a most interesting project and we are very grateful to you in contacting us about it. Yours sincerely, James Currey c.c. Bob Markham

2 December 1970 Markham to Hartwig

Dear Sir: I received a copy of James Currey's letter to you of 24th November and wished to confirm that I am very interested to read the Swahili manuscript of Mr. Kitereza. I look forward to receiving it from you. Yours faithfully, R. C. Markham

9 December 1970 Hartwig to Markham

Dear Mr. Markham,

I was pleased to receive your letter of December 2, 1970 concerning Mr. Kitereza's Swahili manuscript. It is ready for posting but I feel that it may be wise to send it after the current volume of Christmas mail has subsided. At the time of posting in early January I will indicate to you under separate cover how it has been posted. Your interest is appreciated. Sincerely, GWH

21 December 1970 Hartwig to Markham

Dear Mr. Markham,

With reference to your letter of 2nd December 1970, regarding Aniceti Kitereza's Swahili manuscript, it is being posted by air today and I trust it will arrive in your hands shortly.

Pagination is inaccurate in a few instances but I believe the entire manuscript is intact. The duplication of the original presented more than one problem. If any difficulties arise over blurred words in the text please direct the enquiries to me and I will check the original. Mr. Kitereza does not have a copy of the translation in his possession. His address is P.O. Box 16, c/o Kagunguli Parish, Nansio, Ukerewe, Tanzania.

I look forward to hearing from you in the near future.

Sincerely, GWH
cc. Aniceti Kitereza

---

29 December 1970 Markham to Hartwig Dear

Dr. Hartwig,

Aniceti Kitereza' Swahili Manuscript.

Many thanks for your letter of December 21st and for sending me the above manuscript. I am asking my Swahili reader to give me a report on this work and I will let you know what he says. Most sincerely, R. C. Markham

1971

More than forty letters are written between Kitereza, the possible publishers, translators, the Hartwigs and Larson just in this year of 1971. The energy in their exchanges illustrates the commitment and hope that prevails throughout their correspondence.

January 1971 R. Markham (Heinemanns Nairobi to J. Currey, Heinemanns, London

Dear J. Currey:

Re: Bw. Myombekere & Bi. Bugonoka na Ntulanalwo & Bulihwali

I attach John Allen's report (Swahili translator) on the above manuscript which you will remember came to me from Dr. G. W. Hartwig of Duke University, U.S.A.

John is tremendously keen and has asked me to write to Aniceti Kitereza suggesting publication in both English and Swahili. He feels the book is too large to be produced and sold as a single volume and suggests two separate books for each language. The manuscript is in 2 parts, but perhaps we might concentrate on Part I for a start.

John further suggests we ask Kitereza to translate from Swahili to English. If the author refuses, John would oblige.

I must admit that John's keenness is infectious but I would want another opinion here before asking a second reader to report.

I suppose an English translation would be a possibility for the African Writers Series?

Before writing to Kitereza (Dr. Hartwig, please note), I would ask for some comments from you, especially re the English translation. Please write. R. Markham

Reader's Report on Myombekere & Bugonoka (John Allen)

This is something quite out of the ordinary and I am writing after reading no more than a small part of it. I have not the slightest doubt that in English it is a winner, equally readable for fun as fiction, or, seriously as an anthropological study. In Swahili the sales would be slow, because of the inevitable expense of so large a book; but ultimately it will be recognized as a work of great importance, which should unquestionably be in the library of every secondary school. In Kerebe it has not a hope as the reading public is minute; UNLESS it is in western Kerebe, which, if I remember right, is intelligible to Haya and Ganda. This is worth an enquiry.

The Swahili is perhaps a trifle old fashioned; but it is not in my opinion too obviously "dated". It is straightforward and easy and should give no difficulty to any Swahili reader.

You could refuse to commit yourself as a Publisher to Part II until Part I was complete. There is need for haste if you are to have the arrangements completed before the author's death.

Translation into English: If the author does not want to do it, I am prepared to do it, I am prepared to offer my services, provided that I may use tape.

cc. Hartwig, Kitereza

JANUARY 1971 KITEREZA TO LARSON

I wish to thank you for your letter of Dec. 15, 1970 that came with the enclosed check of $15.00. After I opened it, I immediately summoned my wife to come to my side so we could both rejoice together for all your generosity to us. We hope you had a Merry Christmas and an exciting New Year.

The important news here is that the rains came in December as expected. Everybody except the not-too-energetic like us is busy tending their shambas.

I understand you have been reading an interesting book by St. Francis of Asissi. He was a wonderful man. He loved all God's creatures and the world should learn from his great love and do the same.

In your last letter you expressed great joy and surprise that my house had been completed. In a manner of speaking it is but we still have to get the place furnished. There is not much in it except a radio...

Continued...January 6, 1971

Once again I must thank you, Miss Larson, and all your friends with whose help you have done so much for us. I realize you do look forward to obtaining a copy of my book once it is published in English, but I think it would be even be a greater accomplishment if we had the book published both in Swahili and English. I have been asked by several people if my book is being published in Swahili and it is embarrassing to say that it is not.

Now I will tell you about our clothing needs:

2 wool blankets

1 gown for my wife,

1 khanga

2 trousers black

1 black coat

2 shirts   neck size 16 inches

1 pair shoes size 10 for myself

10 Total requirements.

We will appreciate your help in this matter. It is all due to your generosity, otherwise I do not think we could have survived on our own without your help.

It just occurred to me that probably we should have my picture on the book by way of illustration. What do you think about that? Would you tell Jerry about it, too? Thanks. Greetings from Aniceti and Anna Kitereza

---

11 January 1971 Hartwig (North Carolina) to Markham (Kenya)

Dear Mr. Markham:

I am delighted with the response of Professor Allen to Mr. Kitereza's work. Though you directed your question concerning an English translation to Mr. Currey, may I simply add that a quality volume covering the material Kitereza does would fill a tremendous vacuum in the present literature available in English by African authors. Numerous history teachers, like myself, encourage students to read novels by African writers to bridge the gap between academic information and the subjective world of reality.

Even though the market for a Swahili version would be less for the near future, I would think it virtually mandatory, in view of the Tanzanian Department of Education's language policy, to publish it simultaneously in Swahili. There would be a limited market here for the Swahili version as well.

Incidentally, Mr. Kitereza reads English – I correspond with him in it – but he does not speak it to any degree, so you might have to approach

Professor Allen about it. On the other hand, if you would like a German edition, Mr. Kitereza could probably provide a translation! Thanks for keeping me informed. Jerry Hartwig

---

28 JANUARY 1971 KITEREZA TO LARSON

Dear Emilie.

Today I am finding time to write you a short letter! I remember that on 8 January 1971, I sent a letter responding to your Christmas greeting.

Please, Miss Larson, if you wish to continue helping me, please do not send the check of ten US dollars to Dar es Salaam. You must write MWANZA. Please write me concerning this.

These days my legs are very swollen and bother me greatly because during this season of rains I am unable to walk. Greet everyone. AK

---

30 JANUARY 1971 FATHER DESCHAMPS TO HARTWIG

Dear Mr. Hartwig.

Thank you very much for your last letter received 2 days ago. It was indeed a pleasure to hear the good news you sent me about the publication of Aniceti's book. I do hope it will go through without delay.

I went to see Aniceti yesterday. Here is in short what I learned. His health is really not good. It is not only his rheumatism, which he has suffered from even more because of the rains during last months. He also has very bad wounds on his legs which are badly swollen with infection, pain going to his groin. I prepared to take him to hospital but he refused saying that he had already spent a month in Nansio without improvement. I don't know what to do. I wonder how it will turn out.

His house is fine, you would not recognize it, all cemented, good doors and windows and bati roof.

For the work you have, you know the reasons for the delays. He showed me what he had done. He has finished about 107 pages of manuscript. I had not time to read anything but it seems good. He told me he has only about 3 pages more to do before finishing. He promised me to finish it as quickly as possible and to send the book to me. As soon as I get it (it may be any day now) I will send it to you by air- mail. So let's hope for the best. If he delays too much, I'll see him again. If he seems unable to finish it, I will send you what he has already done. It would probably be adequate for your purpose.

Other needs: I gave him money for stamps. He still has enough writing materials. For money, I think he still has something, when I was there he paid a young man who cultivated a nice paddy for him. However, he is hoping you will send him the money you promised as soon as possible. I advise you to do it if you can. He might need it soon for treatments.

Good bye. Greetings from the Fathers here and best regards to Mrs. Hartwig Sincerely R. Deschamp W.F.

---

26 February 1971 Markham – Hartwig

Dear Mr. Hartwig,

Many thanks for your letter of 9th February in which you mention the failing health of the author, Aniceti Kitereza. I am extremely sorry to hear this news, and hope that his local priests can do something for him. You will see from the enclosed copy letter that the manuscript is slow moving, and there have been many delays here since Mr. John Allen made his first quick report. You have obviously had experience in East Africa of similar delays.

At last I have found somebody who is interested in reading the manuscript, and in due course I will let you know what the REO,(Regional Education Officer) Mwanza, thinks about it.

Should I hear of the author's unfortunate demise while we are still deliberating on publication, I feel that this need not stop us from going ahead, should we decide to do so.

Yours sincerely, R. C. Markham

---

26 February 1971 Markham to Regional Education Officer, Mwanza

Dear Sir:

BW. MYOMBEKERE NA BI. BUGONOKA

I refer to your letter reference P/5/II41 of the 13th February, 1971, in which you asked me to send you the manuscript of the above work, so that you could read it and report. You have already received our previous reader's report, and it seems to me that you are interested in this local work.

The manuscript comes in two parts and I am sending it to you under separate registered cover Part I, which can be considered a separate book, and would ask you to go ahead with your reading and reporting.

I would appreciate confirmation in due course that you have safely received the manuscript.

Yours faithfully,
R. C. Markham cc. Mr. GWH

---

1 March 1971 Kitereza to Larson

Dear Ms Emilie Larson

I am delighted to let you know that your letter of February 11, 1979 reached me on Feb. 21, 1971 – Sunday. As I read the letter I was glad to learn that Francis (priest) is still available to help you with translation of my letters that come from this distant island of Ukerewe. I do salute him and thank him for his perception and understanding in helping you and I to communicate without hardship. I wish you, Francis, success with your studies in the U.S.!

It was really touching to hear that David and you often remember me when you talk to one another. I hope you will forward my letter to David.

I am still waiting for that book written on the early inhabitants of America before Columbus discovered the continent. Clyde Jean Baptiste Tripp promised he would send the book in December 1970, but Lo! It's March 1971 and I am still waiting!

I understand you got a letter from Shoonie and something else from Father Deschamps who frequently comes to visit with us.

I am also delighted that you understood my instructions about writing the checks and having them payable in Mwanza.

I wish to let you know that I received your check for $59 dollars on Feb. 23, from Fr. Deschamps himself. I also wish to let you 1know that I received $30 from Jerry after the completion of the synopsis.

I explained to Fr. Deschamps the problems my wife and I are confronted with regarding my illness and hospital visits. I have consequently arranged for a doctor to come to my house where the necessary treatment can be administered.

I hope Jerry is making some progress regarding the publishing of my book. Convey to him my best wishes for success in this endeavor.

I am surprised that the winter has been so long and cold. Remember me to David and all your other friends whose kindness we highly appreciate. God bless you. A.K

9 MARCH 1971 FR DESCHAMPS TO HARTWIG

Dear Mr. Hartwig,

Thank you so much for your last letter and for the cheques you sent. Special thanks for the $10 you sent me. I am very grateful for that help.

Sorry for the delay in answering you; please excuse me. It is not pure neglect. Since the beginning of February, I have been very busy with baptism preparations and since the 1st of March with special Lent instruction for girls. On top of that the weather has been very hot and therefore tiring.

However, the day after receiving your cheques, I went to see Aniceti and brought him the money = 623/- for $30 from you and $59 from Miss Larson. If by chance I receive more than that from the bank, I can give him the difference later on. I suppose you got that news from Aniceti. No need to say he was very glad to receive that money. I was also happy to see that he is much better. At least his wounds were cured. He got penicillin injections from somebody?? And that did the trick. That made me wonder what kind of treatment he got in Bukonge Hospital? For his rheumatism, I don't think there is much to be done.

With the money, he wants to buy some blankets (warm ones) and a sweater. He assured me that he could manage to get them and since I had so much work, I was not displeased to leave the matter in his hands.

So I hope everything is o.k. with him for the time being. I'll keep an eye on him from time to time. And if there is anything else I can do for you, I'll be pleased to oblige.

Good-bye. My best regards to Mrs. Hartwig. Sincerely, R. Deschamps. W.F

5 APRIL 1971 MARKHAM TO HARTWIG

Dear Mr. Hartwig,

Re: BW MYOMBEKERE NA BI BUGANOKA

I am going through the usual frustration of dealing with officials within the Tanzanian administration and so much time has been wasted because of their indifference and what seems to be a complete lack of interest in Swahili writing.

I simply must obtain another reading just in case Mr. John Allen's first reading was a little biased, and as this book has so much intrinsic value to the developing country of Tanzania, I must receive the green light from its Government.

This letter merely puts you in the picture and as soon as I have something positive I will advise you. Yours Sincerely, R. Markham

---

4 MAY 1971 KITEREZA TO HARTWIGS

Dear Bwana and Mama Hartwig!

I am sending greetings to all in your family. I received your letter of March 9, 1971 on April 1 in the evening. When I opened the envelope, I discovered a very nice picture of you and your children. It is a very nice picture and my wife, Anna, and I are happy to see your youngest laughing. Thank you, thank you!

You wrote that you have now received the synopsis of my book. A asked a relative to take it to Father Deschamps to mail as I do not have the money. I hope you have received it. Father Deschamps came to my home on 18 April 1971, a Sunday. We talked and he told me that in Durham you have snow! We also talked about E. Larson who asked for a statement about my health.

You asked if I have bought some clothes that I requested from E. Larson but here, these items are very expensive. I have bought blankets. I kept some money to give the doctors. My rheumatism is in my whole body and so I have little strength and trouble walking. The medicine is so so. I have received several injections and two bottles of medicine named: Special PARIS microcrystalline – Procaine-Penicillin – suspension in oil containing 2% of aluminium monostearate – shake before use.

The money from the synopsis which you sent I used to hire a young man to help in our farming plot. As yet we have no rains so planting might not still reap fruit.

Goodbye to all of you, my friends, in Durham. P.S. A blessed Easter Sunday. A.K.

MAY 1971 MARKHAM TO HARTWIG

Dr. Mr. Hartwig,

Many thanks for your recent letter with which you enclosed your proposed introduction to Aniceti Kitereza's novel which you have prepared for Research in African Literatures.

I still have the same sad story to tell you regarding the fate of the two halves of Kitereza's Swahili work. The Regional Education Officer, Mwanza has had the first half for the last three months and refuses to answer letters and to return the manuscript with his report.

The Institute of Swahili Research in Dar es Salaam has had the second part for approximately the same length of time and although they have acknowledged receipt and have stated that they are working on it, I can get no further information from them.

I realize that Kitereza's health is gradually getting worse and I am doing my personal best in trying to establish if this publishing house can possibly publish his Swahili work.

I am certain that you will realize that an evaluation must come from a Tanzanian source for such a work.

May I congratulate you and your wife on the tone of the introduction and I can assure you that it does not infringe in any way upon my interests in this Author.

Yours sincerely,

R. C. Markham

---

21 MAY 1971 KITEREZA TO LARSON

Greetings to you.

I remember that the statement I received from Kagunguli Hospital on 17 May 1971 seems to be lost. I cannot find it. But I will try to recount to you the history of my health which I will recall from 16 September 1956. I had been working in my small farm as it was just before the rainy season. As usual, I began in the morning and worked until night. After bathing, I went to visit friends and stayed with them until early evening.

And then I began to ache and it felt like my legs had a great weight. It was so bad that when I tried to stand up from the chair where I was sitting, suddenly- I fell down, right on my face. Loo!!

I couldn't get up by myself, I had no strength and I couldn't stand by myself. My friends helped me back to my home. Since that day, my legs continue to swell causing me to move very slowly!! The muscles in my legs and arms continue to bother me from morning til night and when it is cold, it is worse.

Again, in the year 1956, our traditional doctors (African-magic) came to see me and after drawing blood, said it was too dark, black even like a cooking pot. Then in January 1957, a white doctor came to Kagunguli hospital. My family asked him to see me and I stayed there six months. The doctor said, "Indeed, you suffer in your legs but also your heart is not well. We will try to give you medicines to make you well."

And so, since I left the hospital, the swelling in my legs continues so that I cannot walk far. And when it is cold, I cough from morning til night. So this is the history of my health.

Thank you again for your letter and picture. Greet David and the Hartwigs. Yours, Mzee A.Kitereza

---

2 JUNE 1971 MARKHAM TO HARTWIG

Dear Mr. Hartwig,

Further to my letter of 20th May, I have now heard from the Institute of Swahili Research in Dar es Salaam re Part II of Aniceti's work which was sent to them for analysis several months ago.

I quote from their report dated 24th May:

"The Institute of Kiswahili has read critically the manuscript all through and felt that the theme running through is interesting and makes an exciting reading.

However the language does not conform to the acceptable standard of Swahili in many respects; and this in general has spoilt the whole work. Because the construction mistakes have marred the whole book, it is extremely necessary to re-write the whole story again if you insist on publishing it."

John Allen, who was and still is tremendously keen, noted that the Swahili "is perhaps a trifle old-fashioned but not too dated." The Institute says the Swahili does not conform. Two conflicting reports from recognized authorities.

Publication is still the risk of the Publisher but the Institute's report is something of a deterrent to publishing as it is obvious that Aniceti cannot rewrite throughout.

I am still waiting for the report on the first part from the Regional Education Officer, Mwanza. When this is received (I remind him twice per month), I will evaluate the whole and let you know the outcome.

I am sorry this has taken so long but Tanzania is the obvious market for such a book, hence my decision to send the two halves to Tanzanian experts for opinions and advice. Yours sincerely, R.C. Markham

---

7 JUNE 1971 HARTWIG TO MARKHAM

Dear Mr. Markham.

Thank you for your letter of 2nd June.

The response of the Institute of Kiswahili to Aniceti's Swahili is not surprising. It is undoubtedly a fair assessment; secondary school pupils on Ukerewe who read sections of the story make similar remarks.

I am encouraged by the Institute's response concerning the content. This is our particular concern which is presumably shared by Mr. Allen. I am confused, however, by the comment that "it is extremely necessary to rewrite the whole story again if you insist on publishing it." (The word "insist" comes rather strongly.) As a language institute they are naturally concerned about promoting standard Swahili rather than literature, but "to rewrite the whole story"…does this mean to edit the manuscript?

This would be my interpretation and, if this is the case, would this be a major endeavor?

Aniceti is well aware that his Swahili emanates from an earlier era. There is little he can do about that dilemma. I think he would consent to editing revisions that would make the language conform to that desired by the Institute. I feel that the content is too valuable to permit an inflexible response to the Institute's criticism. I have attempted in the past two years to prepare Aniceti for the possibility that revisions might be necessary; he is just as sensitive about his work as the next writer.

Thank you for keeping me informed. Sincerely, Gerald Hartwig

---

14 JUNE 1971 ALLEN TO MARKHAM

Dear Bob,

Prof. Hartwig has kindly sent me a copy of his letter to you dated 7 June. I am sending him a copy of this. Within a month I shall make a determined effort to visit the Institute of Swahili Research and find out what they do mean. The extracts from their report remind me of the reports sent out by the (then wholly European) Swahili committee in the thirties. There is no conflict between their assessment and mine. It is possible that Aniceti's Swahili does not conform with some rigid rules to which the Institute has decided to adhere. It certainly does not conform with the rigid rules of the old committee—nor did the works of the late Shaaban Robert, to which I used to give the approval of the committee by return of post, before I had read them. If the Institute proposes to pour all new Swahili work into a rigid mould, there will be no development of Swahili literature until their views change Let us settle down to rewriting Shakespeare, Jane Austen and Amos Tutuola into Standard English. You have seen the same thing done (very badly) to Desturi za Masuaheli and you have seen comments on this by competent Swahili critics. It is authors who can write that make a literary language, not grammarians who think that they know what is wrong.

I must apologize to you: you know that I have been and am badly rushed and I had not read your letter of 2 June with sufficient care. Professor Hartwig's reply forced me to bring it to the top of the pile and to realize that there is a serious problem to be faced. This will probably mean spending an extra two days in Dar es Salaam. I think it can be crammed in and you may expect to hear from me before long.

To edit the manuscript to force it to conform with some arbitrary rules would be more than a "major endeavour". It would be a work of the utmost futility and a crime against all literary canons. Yours sincerely, John Allen

---

1ᴴ June 1971 Markham to D. M. Neale Science Research Associates, Oxfordshire U.K.

Dear Mr. Neale.

My local office (Heinemanns-Nairobi, Kenya) is actually and actively publishing, mostly in the Swahili medium and mostly translations from English of our famous African Writers series.

The work has spread and I am regularly receiving manuscripts in both English and Swahili, some original, some translations, offers from translators and all manner of literary work, most of which is immature and not worthy of publication.

However, one manuscript arrived here recently which I feel deserves a special mention which your committee may wish to consider for an award under the Margaret Wrong Fund.

The author is Aniceti Kitereza and he was "discovered" by Dr. Gerald W. Hartwig. His work translated into Swahili is called Bwana Myombekere Na Bibi Bugonoka Na Ntulanalwo na Bulihwali and sooner than spell out the full story here, I enclose various copies of letters, reports, etc. which are self-explanatory.

Aniceti's health is failing and a priest attached to a nearby mission told me in January, "His health is really not good. It is not only his rheumatism… but his very bad leg wounds which are badly swollen with infection, the pain going to his groin. I offered to take him to hospital but he refused saying he had already spent a month in hospital with no improvement."

The Institute of Swahili Research on Part II of his Swahili manuscript expressed the opinion that it would be "extremely necessary to rewrite the whole story before publication." Both Hartwig and John Allen (probably the world's leading Swahili scholar) are aghast at this and have both objected. In a recent letter from John Allen he informs me he is visiting Dar es Salaam shortly and will call on the Director of the Institute in order to find out what they mean. He says that to edit Aniceti's M.S. to force it to conform with some arbitrary rules would be more than a major endeavour. It would be a work of the utmost futility and a crime against all literary canons.

Part I of Aniceti's M.S. is still with the Regional Education officer, Mwanza, Tanzania, who has kept it so long despite constant reminders to return it

Regarding publication, I am unsure and would need more advice on the Swahili content and deeper thought on publishing both English and Swahili editions.

The object of this letter is not to ask you to consider my publishing house for a grant under the Fund in order to publish but to ask you to think of this poor and sick author, who is nearing the end of his years to whom a cash gift at this stage would not only improve his health but would do greater help by boosting his literary ego. If he is forced by the Institute to rewrite his Swahili, he will deserve a grant.

If you require further details, please let me know. Yours sincerely, R.C. Markham

---

2 JULY 1971 MARKHAM TO ALLEN

BW MYOMBEKERE NA BI BUGONOKA Na NTULAMALWO Na BULIHWALI

Dear John:

Part I was returned by the Regional Education Officer, Mwanza. His covering letter was written on 30th April, altered to 23rd May, posted surface mail June 2nd and received by cleft stick here today.

He states that due to pressure of work he is unable to read it and cannot give an opinion. It was sent in mid-February, a complete waste of 4½ months.

I was naturally waiting for a report from a possible expert living in and responsible for the area in which Aniceti lives but nothing emerged.

What have I now? Your opinion that it is something quite out of the ordinary, that its Swahili is somewhat old-fashioned but straightforward, that it would start selling slowly but would eventually catch on. Hartwig's sincere opinion is that it must be published. The Institute of Swahili Research's opinion that if it is published it would be necessary to rewrite the whole story.

I must soon make up my mind about publication of the Swahili edition. Its length of 876 handwritten pages tends to put me off and I dislike a two-

part edition. As its market will be predominantly Tanzania, I must make it a cheap edition at grass-roots price and this would be impossible at its present length, either in one volume or two.

In your letter of 14th June you mention your determined effort to visit the Institute in July asking them what they mean by their report. I have not thanked you for this but hasten to thank you now. If you convince them (and I am sure you will!) that the book need not be re-written into modern Swahili, I still have the problem of its length.

Could its two parts be compressed into one? Would the editing out affect the whole work? Would it lose its literary value by halving it? Who would do the work? I am certain the author could and would not and I know you are far too busy.

Before you go to Dar es Salaam to take up battle stations perhaps you would ponder over my problem of length. I do not want a decision but advise you to not write before your trip but no doubt you will wait to write after your trip.

The English edition is another matter and if it is as good as Dr Hartwig states, it ought to fill a number in the African Writers Series. Perhaps Dr. Hartwig, or the author, would inform me who has the original English manuscript. I think I was told it was 300 pages of typescript. I am prepared to read it if it is sent to me and then, possibly, sent it on to London where all the A.W.S. is published.

Some time ago, Dr. Hartwig said that publication of both the English and Swahili edition would be virtually mandatory in view of the Tanzania History of Education's language policy. Being a little bitter at the moment, I doubt his words. I doubt if there exists a language policy in Tanzania. Their reactions to Swahili language in literature are negative, their attitudes in analyzing Swahili manuscripts lazy and unproductive and their recommendations of published Swahili works practically nil.

Best wishes. Enjoy yourself in Bagamoyo and don't lose your temper nor your way in Mgulani Street, Dar es Salaam.

Sincerely, R.C. Markham cc: Hartwig and Kitereza

---

25 June 1971 Hartwig to Markham

Dear Mr. Markham,

Bw. Myombekere na Bi. Bugonoka

A copy of your letter to Mr. D M. Neale concerning Aniceti Kitereza was received yesterday. Needless to say, I was somewhat overwhelmed by your endeavors on his behalf – and very pleased. His literary efforts, of course, must stand on their own merits, but to recommend him for consideration for an award under the Margaret Wong Fund is to consider him as an author and as a literary contributor to his people. It is a marvelous gesture. I only hope that you have the opportunity of meeting him. He has that endearing, warm quality of appreciating and enjoying life in spite of its ordeals.

Incidentally, the letter that John Allen sent to you earlier this month boosted my morale noend.

Best wishes, Gerald Hartwig

---

5 July 1971 Markham to Hartwig

Dear Dr. Hartwig

Bw. Myombekere na Bi. Bugonoka

Thank you for your letter of the 25th June. I have had a reply from Mr. D.M. Neale of the Margaret Wrong Memorial Fund, who answers:

"Many thanks for your letter of June 17 and all the enclosures. I raised this with the committee, who wrote me a day or two after I received it, and though they were very sympathetic to the idea, they were not at present prepared to consider the use of the fund for such a purpose, since there seem to be alternative possibilities that merit equal consideration and further research.

It was worth a try, and as Mr. Neale is coming to Nairobi in August, I can discuss it with him further.

Yours sincerely, R.C. Markham

---

5 July 1971 Father Deschamps to Hartwig

Dear Mr. Hartwig.

Thanks for your letter which I received on the 1st July when I came back from safari. I also found letters from Mr. Markham explaining difficulties about Aniceti's manuscript and asking for my help in recovering Part I from the R.E.O. Mwanza.

Since I am just back from Mwanza, I can't afford to take 3 days off again to go to see the R.E.O. Secondly, I find it useless to write him myself. I thought Aniceti could present a stronger case and have more influence. So I went to see Aniceti immediately, Thursday p.m. and again, Saturday a.m. He promised me to write to the R.E.O.

Secondly, I wrote to Mr. Markham and suggested that, if he does not receive manuscript soon, he should send a strong reminder with copy to Minister of Education and threats of legal action against him.

I do hope he recovers the manuscript soon and that things can be fixed up for its publication. However, I see difficulties for the Swahili version; the Swahili Research Institute is going in only for very high brow Swahili of the coast type. A simple, easily understood Swahili is no good for them.

Aniceti is well enough these days. The dry weather is favorable to him. Both days I found him in his rice paddy chasing birds. He complains of having lost money, around 200/Tsh which he paid to have his shamba cultivated. However, I saw a bag of rice in his house and there is still a lot more to be reaped in the paddy. So it should not be such a complete loss.

Good-bye. Greetings to Mrs. Hartwig. Sincerely, R. Deschamps W.F.

---

12 July 1971 Hartwig to Markham

Dear Mr. Markham:

I received your letter to John Allen today and I could only sigh in response to it. Our 'friend' in Mwanza rather let the side down!

I hasten, however, to clarify the matter of the original manuscript – if you have aspirin nearby you might have it ready. The original manuscript is in Kikerebe which is still possibly in Aniceti's possession; an English version is non-existent. If I am not mistaken, I mentioned this earlier, hence Mr. Allen's original response indicating that he would be willing to translate it into English.

I am beginning to share your misgivings about a Swahili version, but what a shame! Sincerely, Gerald Hartwig

---

14 July 1971 Markham to Kitereza

Bw. Myombekere na Bi. Bugonoka Dear Bw. Kitereza,

I wrote to Mr. John Allen on 2nd July and sent a copy of my letter to you so you are in the picture regarding the possibility of publication of your work in Swahili.

I have recently spoken to Mr. John Allen, who is visiting Nairobi, and he is of the opinion that the manuscript in English does not exist, whereas I feel that it does. In my letter of 2nd July I asked both you and Dr. Hartwig if the English manuscript did exist and where it was, but to date I have not received a reply from either of you.

If no English manuscript exists, Mr. John Allen is prepared to translate the Swahili manuscript into English, but insists that he does this translation on tape as he has no time to put in type-script.

He suggests that in the beginning he translates one or two chapters of your Swahili work and then sends it on tape to you. This means, of course, that you would have to have access to a tape-recorder If you possess such an instrument, would you please tell me at what speeds it works, and if you do not possess one, is it possible for you to borrow one locally, again informing me of the speeds.

I suggest that if you agree to this method of translation, you listen to the first part of Mr. Allen's translation and you then advise if it is acceptable to you. Then, we may go ahead with the English translation and perhaps would publish it in this English form in our African Writers Series.

I must stress that this is not a promise of publication, as there are so many unknowns, but I can assure you that if you like the idea, there is a possibility that we may go ahead. However I would have to have the backing of my London office before so doing.

With reference to the Swahili manuscript, you will have read my letter of 2nd July outlining the difficulties, especially in respect of advice received from the Institute of Swahili Research in Dar es Salaam, and because of its length, but we feel here that if the English edition is published there should follow a demand for the Swahili work, and I feel this is now the obvious way to tackle this.

May I please have your answers as soon as possible. With best wishes,

Yours Sincerely, R.C.Markham cc. Dr. Hartwig John Allen

July 30 1971 Kitereza to Larson

Dear Miss Emilie:

My heart is filled with happiness to have an opportunity to give you replies to your two letters received on June 9 and June 20, 1971. As you say, the weeks go by quickly if you are a healthy person, but if you are ill and surrounded by pains day and night, eee! For you are not able to determine the rate of speed of day and night because of the many pains of the sickness.

I understand that in April you spoke with Mr. Hartwig about Ukerewe and a publisher for my book. And, I read that you have sent me medicine by air. Thank you so much for the gift. I shall take the tablets just as prescribed.

Kind regards from my wife Anna and I. We with you happiness and good health, your life in this earth be a long one and our Lord guide you from any kind of harm or bad accident. Give my regards to the family of David

It is us here who are yours, lady, and you love you always. A. Kitereza and Mrs. Kitereza

---

30 July 1971 Kitereza to Hartwig

Dear Hartwig!

Your letter of 22 June 1971, I received on July 4, 1971 on Sunday. You told me about news from Mr. Markham, the manager of Heinemanns in Nairobi that the section I translated to Kiswahili was sent to the head office, Regional Educational Officer in Mwanza. In addition, Father Deschamps came here on 3 July 1971 with letters from Markham and what he wrote to the REO.

Father Deschamps told me that Markham, a white man, tried to get answers from the REO regarding my writing. Mr. Markham wrote letters on 25 March, 23 April, 18 May and 2 June hoping for an answer.

Father R. Deschamps told me that as the Tanzanian writer of the manuscript that I send a request to Mwanza.. Without delay, I began with my pen to write. Again on 9 July 1971 on Friday evening, I received a copy of the letter from Markham which he copied to John Allen, Esq. saying that the REO, Mwanza, returned my manuscript after four and a half months. Loo!

And so, Bwana Dr. Hartwig, I do not see how these proceedings will continue with my writing. I have translated from Kikerebe to Kiswahili the opening sections. But now there is a request for an English translation for African Writers Series.

I would write more but I have no more stamps or money. Greetings to Mama Shoonie and the children and to you. A.Kitereza

---

20 August 1971 Markham to Hartwig

Dear Mr. Hartwig: Bw. Myombekere na Bi. Bugonoka

I find that I have not answered your letter of 12th July, especially your handwritten foot-note in which you mention Mr. Anza Lema as an alternative reader of Aniceti's Swahili manuscript.

I prefer to keep him up my sleeve, as at the moment we have decided to press on which a possible English version of this book, translated and edited by Mr. John Allen.

This decision has been arrived at rather reluctantly, but the Swahili version is far too long to appear as a book, as its length will automatically push up its price and we will lose most of the market for which it is so obviously designed

If the English edition is pubished and catches on, we will then give second thoughts to a Swahili edition. This is how matters stand at the moment.

I have had two letters from Aniceti recently, and he seems to agree with the idea of an English translation in the first place.

Yours sincerely, R. C. Markham

---

20 August 1971 Markham to Allen

Dear John:

BW. MYOMBEKERE NA BI. BUGONOKA

I enclose two recent letters from Mr Aniceti Kitereza and a further letter from Father Deschamps, all of which I feel sure would interest you.

I get the impression that Aniceti is rather scared of your idea of vetting your Engish translation on tape, and I further gather that both the holy father and the author are against the idea of a tape procedure.

How would you feel about taking the responsibility of a translation from the Swahili on to tape without sending such tapes to the author for approval? I seems that everybody wants to trust us to make a good translation and I am sure that you will read this into Aniceti's letters

Before I go any further, would you please let me know how you feel and if you are still interested in doing a translation, the tapes of which could be sent here and we could get a local secretarial bureau to do the typing. Please return the three letters with your reply.

Yours sincerely, R.C. Markham cc. Dr. Gerald Hartwig

---

3 September 1971 Markham to Allen

BW. MYOMBEKERE na BI. BUGONOKA

Thank you for your letter of 26th August.

I am certain we all greatly appreciate your offer to visit Ukerewe with your wife in late September with the intention of speaking to the author, and discussing the translation into English of Aniceti's Swahili work.

I have heard from Father Deschamps that he has received your letter and has replied to it.

Noted that after spending a few days with the author you will come to Nairobi and discuss the project with me.

I am sending you under separate cover the first half of Aniceti's tome into which you can sink your teeth and get onto tape as much as you have time for. The speed of our tape is 1 7/8 l.p.m. You have kindly offered to translate on to tape a few chapters which you will send to me for typing. I will then send the type-script of your translation to the author at Ukerewe in time for your arrival there. I sincerely hope our timing is perfect.

Re your word on wills, Father Deschamps has sent me a copy of Aniceti's will. I gather you may wish to discuss this with both Father Deschamps and Aniceti when you visit them.

Many thanks for your help, and for your wife's encouragement. Yours sincerely, R.C. Markham

---

14 OCTOBER 1971 KITEREZA TO LARSON

Dear Emilie Larson!

I am very sorry but since you sent me medicine, it is now finished. I wrote a letter of thanks when I received it on 1 August 1981 but I have yet to receive your answer. In my heart, I am thinking: "Perhaps the letter I sent you with thanks you never received?"

But I have received a letter from Mrs. Shoonie, wife of Dr. Gerald J. Hartwig in Durham, North Carolina that you sent me very good medicine and so I believe you did receive my letter.

Really, Miss Larson, this medicine is excellent for my cough, for me and my wife Anna and now, the cough is gone! So I ask you please to send more!

Mr. Markham of Nairobi Publisher of my book sent Mr. John Allen and his wife. They visited us here on 28/29 September 1971. Mr. Allen is translating my book into English!

I don't have many words today; my wife Anna sends greetings! Greet David and his mother and father. Your friend, AK

---

29 OCTOBER 1971 MARKHAM TO HARTWIG

Dear Dr. Hartwig: BW. MYOMBEKERE NA BI. BUGONOKA-Kitereza

The enclosed will enlighten you. I am sorry I have been silent lately. John Allen says he saw Aniceti with a copy of TRIBUS dated 18.8.1969 in which you did an article on Kerebe sculpture. The article was backed up by plates, and if this thing goes ahead, we might wish to include some of your illustrations in the book.

Presumably the editor of TRIBUS holds the rights for the article? Would you help by finding this out? If he holds the rights for the article would he also 'own' the plates? What about reproduction fees?

As you can see, we have dropped the Swahili idea but it is in limbo, not completely dead.

Best wishes to you and I look forward to hearing from you.

Yours sincerely, R.C. Markham cc: John Allen (copy of the following letter enclosed with above)

---

20 OCTOBER 1971 MARKHAM TO CURRY (HEINEMANNS, LONDON)

cc: Alan Hill/Keith Sambrook (Heinemanns London) John Allen, Arusha, TZ, Gerald Hartwig, USA

Dear James,

BW MYOMBEKERE na BI BUGONOKA – Aniceti Kitereza

The above book has a long history. It is in two phases – Swahili and English. It will, I hope, have a different title on publication.

It was first brought to our attention by Gerald Hartwig (Xerox copy of his letter to you of October 27th 1970 attached). Later, he sent me photocopies of the manuscript in the author's handwriting in Swahili.

John Allen was consulted and after months of correspondence between author, author's friend and adviser (a Catholic priest at the Nansio Mission, Hartwig, Allen, various Swahili experts and bodies, and this office, it was decided to scrap the Swahili version and conentrate on the English.

It was obvious that communication was our biggest headache so John Allen very kindly went out of his way to visit Aniceti Kitereza a few weeks ago which meant driving over rough roads and corrugations, crossing antiquated ferries and living roughly. John was not commissioned to make this trip. His interest in the Swahili edition of the book and its contents gave him an urge to meet the author.

Aniceti is a very old man, crippled with arthritis, but game for many more years of life. His wife is old and frail and John fears she will go first. Once she goes, he goes. All their children have died. He has no heir. He is very, very poor. (see Hartwig's notes on the author attached.)

John and Aniceti conversed in Swahili but the author prefers to write in German or French, not English. They had long talks about the book. John was not carrying any brief whatsoever from me, but on his return from safari, he suggested the following.

H.E.B. contracts the author (probably commissions is a better word at this stage) for an English edition giving him three royalty options, a) outright purchase of his rights, b) part purchase, part royalty, c) usual full royalty. a) could be offered as Aniceti may not live long and has no heir. However, he may smell a rat, hence b).

John Allen had recent political difficulties with the estate of the Swahili writer, the late Shabaan Robert, so in THIS contract he would like to be mentioned as Translator/Editor with a specific fixed fee of one shilling. Outside the contract, he would accept his expenses but rejects a fee. He enjoys the work and has a high regard for the author. His expenses would be fair and reasonable.

John will translate Aniceti's Swahili on to tape into English. This office will put into typescript. He will send us tapes from time to time and we type 4 copies, sending 3 copies to John. He corrects all, sends two to Aniceti who confirms, keeping on and returning one to John. John then sends it on to me. John has already begun translation. We have already begun typing from tape.

We feel the Swahili 850 pages of foolscap long-hand will be reduced. The Editor will make a point of reducing further by editing out unimportant parts of the story. I am guessing at a final length of 450 pages.

We all have faith in and enthusiasm for this book and I personally feel it could make the African Writers Series. Our idea is for the book to make a success of its English edition and then think of a possible Swahili edition.

It will take John Allen a very long time to translate finally and complete the editing. I cannot therefore send you a manuscript but I enclose a few pages from the first chapter which are not in final perfect manuscript form. They might give you an idea of the style and content.

I suppose you can call this letter a "feeler" as it cannot be a firm publishing proposal owing to lack of a manuscript.

Your colleague, Keith Sambrook, recently spent a week with us and has seen the idea in formation and has witnessed our keenness. He could not see a manuscript as there isn't one. He may have some ideas on the book for discussion with you when he returns to London. Arising from his visit is the possibility that this office may spread its publishing wings and if the London board agree with his proposals, we may be able to take on this book if you in London reject it. Bearing in mind that any overseas publishing proposal has to have London's blessing first, this is not to be taken as any form of blackmail. I would naturally like you to think in terms of A.W.S. not a small overseas local production.

Your initial reactions will be very welcome.
Yours sincerely, R.C.Markham

Enclosure of beginning translation of Myombekere and Bugonoka by John Allen (This is the original, rough draft translation)
Chapter 1. M. is robbed of his wife B.

M and B were married after completing all the requirements of the law and custom of marriage. They were still young. A year went by and in the second year B. became pregnant but her pregnancy lasted for 4 months only and in the fifth month she miscarried a male child. A short time later his wife became pregnant for a second time and this pregnancy continued for six months but in the seventh month again she lost her baby which was a daughter. The child lived for one day only and on the second day left this world. After that M.'s wife did not become pregnant again and they lived for many years childless.

Now M's relations began to be vexed and irresponsibly advised him to put away his wife. They said, you are our brother, are you content to live with this your wife childless and to allow your personality to lost in the grave? How do you imagine that people live again? Is it not by having children and leaving seed that is alive? This is the way in which your clan goes on. If your father and mother had had not children, where would you have come from? No man is barren; he can cure himself and the cure for a man is to take his bow and to go to seek a wife. If you seek a wife and get married at your age, ou cannot fail to have children.

M. replied, What is it that you want me to do?

His relations said, we want you to put away your wife and to marry another because if you live with her you are not likely to get a child.

What they were saying was very soon heard by the family of M's wife. When they heard that the family wanted to reject their daughter, Nam, his father-in-law,and Nkwanzi, his mother-in-law were very angry and made up their minds to go and bring their child home.

They started off at sunrise and, because they lived a long way off, they made haste so as to arrive in the morning and be able to return the same day. On the way they talked together and Nkwanzi said, "When we arrive at the homestead of our son in law, how can we express ourselves strongly enough to persuade them to allow us to take away our daughter?"

Nam replied to his wife, "What queer ideas you women do have; it is obvious that there is not the slightest difficulty. Do not consider, my dear wife, that the way in which they have treated our daughter Buganoka is sufficient to show that they completely reject her. Just as a man throws down a heavy load of firewood, they have rejected her and it is clear that they have rejected her, and all this is because your child is an utter fool.

She is not a child at all, if she were she would be able to bear a child, and now she has had a miscarriage and a second miscarriage. Should she not have borne two children? Now because of her stupidity and ignorance she has nothing whatsoever to say and all the insults that they pour upon her have no effect on her. If she has as much sense as you she would already have gone away and we should have returned to our son in law the bride price which we paid long ago. By now undoubtedly we should have got her married to somebody else. Do not worry, my dear wife, if you want to say anything, think first, and then say it openly. Probably when we reach our son in law's homestead, first we shall have a little rest, and they will take from us our weapons,

(Footnote: Weapons: In the old days it was customary for all men when journeying from one place to another to carry weapons such as a spear and bow and arrows to protect themselves from enemies and animals.)

and give us stools to sit on so that we may greet them properly in a friendly manner giving the impression that we are stupid and to not know what is going on. We will not plunge into the subject standing up as if we were Jita folk. I think I had better do the talking because you will first go into your daughter's house and there you will have a look round and explain to her clearly that we have come to take her away back to our own homestead. You will say to her: I will stop here because you know better than we do. It is clear to us that your husband's family have rejected you entirely. Does not this distress you? Are you going to wait until they throw out your magic horns and your sifting basket to show you that they reject you? So we have come today to take you away. When you have spoken to her like this, then raise your voice and say: Namwero, why do not we go away; are you going to spend the night here? Then I will call them all together and tell them that we want to go at once. We will not say anything to slow things up, as though we wanted to be friendly to them and pay them compliments.

When they came near to the area where their son in law had his home, they went to ease themselves in the bushes at the side of the path which they were following, because they had started out very early and had gone through paths covered with dew in the rain and had forded several deep rivers, and the dew and the river water had given them diarrhoea. They reached their son in law's homestead at eleven in the morning and before they went into the yard of the homestead where they were still in the Rukongo, that is the road leading to the homestead lined on both sides with trees to prevent domestic animals damaging the plants or growing crops which were cultivated at that time, they came upon Myombekere's young niece playing near the main entrance to the homestead. When she saw them, she said: Hi, uncle, some people are coming.

When M. looked at the gate, he saw that it was his father-in-law. As he hastened to go to welcome him and as he had gone a little way, he looked again and saw that his mother-in-law was there too, so he immediately turned away so that he should not meet her fact to face, and his mother-in-law too, stood there at the entrance of the homestead.

Then M. called his wife, who was in the house washing the potatoes which she had lifted from the field by the river. Buganoka, Buganoka! and his wife answered, Sir? Bugonoka, bring stools and the weapons from your guests.

The reason why M. hastily called his wife to come with stools and to take the weapons from his guests was this: he was shy of taking his father-in-law's weapons when his hands were dirty, because he had woken very early, and had been busy boiling and drying the meat of a dead calf belonging to some people who had given it to him to look after. When the meat was dry, he would take it to the owner of the beast. The calf had died suddenly in the homestead.

He was shy of taking his father-in-law's weapons when his hands were covered with fat and soot. Secondly, he was anxious not to surprise his mother-in-law, because according to Kerebe custom, they should always avoid each other. The mother-in-law avoids her son-in-law and the son-in-law avoids his mother-in-law. This is good manners throughout Kerebe.

So when B. came out of the house she was smiling with joy at seeing the guests whom her husband had charged her to greet. They were her own father and mother and B. was delighted to see them. She saw who was there and it did not matter who was not there. She took her father's weapons and asked her mother to come into the homestead, for her husband had taken himself away while he was drying the meat of the calf.

After welcoming her mother in the house, B. hastily snatched up her stool and took it to her father outside in the shade of a tree, called Omutoma, near the place where his son-in-law was working. When her father had sat down, he asked his daughter to bring him some water to drink. B. went into the house and took a ladle, brushed the dust off it and opened and uncovered the water pot and quickly drew some water to take to him.

As she approached her father she curtsied to him politely and gave it to him with both hands. Her father received the ladle, which was full of very sweet water. He drank and gulped it down and then poured on the ground the half that remained in the ladle. The chickens immediately came to drink it, bending down their beaks and stretching out their necks as is their way. When Namwero had poured out the the remainder of the water he took a deep breath – Yahoo!

His daughter asked him, Father, why did you drink that water so eagerly? Her father replied, At home, my daughter, last night until nearly light, we were drinking banana beer and perhaps, too, the dew has got into our limbs.

Then she greeted her father, saying "malama" and her father received his daughter saying "Mangunu", meaning "Peace be with you".

After this, Myombekere too greeted his father-in-law saying "Kempire sumalama" and his father-in- law received his greetings of a whole year or several years without having met, saying "Tenguni, Lata". When they had exchanged greetings and asked each other all the news, and how people were getting on here and elsewhere, M. got up to go greet his mother-in-law who had gone into the house of her daughter B.

When he came nearer the door of the house (Footnote: Houses of those days skillfully built and fitted the door with something like an umbrella to keep off rain or sun and thatched from the top right down to the ground.) He skirted the wall according to the custom of the country so that he should not meet his mother-in-law face to face. He then knelt down, turned away on the left outside the house, because he knew that his mother-in-law would be on that side. For according to Kerebe custom an honoured guest is received and given a stool to sit upon there because there is placed soft leaves like a mattress and, because she was unable to sit down, she had stretched herself out on the stool.

He squatted down and greeted his mother humbly: "How have you slept, Mother?" and his mother-in-law received his greeting, saying, "We are well, my son." They exchanged news but without meeting face to face; they could converse, but they could not see each other.

1 November 1971 Hartwig to Markham

Dear Mr. Markham,

Thank you for your letter and enclosures of October 20th. Your silence is never disturbing so long as good news follows in its wake!

I am awed by Mr. Allen's safari to Ukerewe to visit Aniceti, particularly if he went through the Serengeti from Arusha. I gather from your letter to Mr. Curry that Mr. Allen regarded the discomfort as justified; I trust his wife concurred! Words fail to convey my appreciation for the Allens' concern and efforts.

Aniceti informed me just before your letter arrived that the Allens had visited him. He was in good spirits but, as always, quiet about financial affairs, except his need for postage stamps. (I am sure John Allen either left stamps with him or money for them. Poverty and immobility can present real problems at times.)

A copy of my letter to Dr. J. Zwernemann is enclosed as well as an off-print of the article. Some of them may be useful. I do know that Aniceti is insistent upon having illustrations in his book. I have informed him on more than one occasion that novels do not always have them. But he has not accomplished what he has in his circumstances by listening to mundane comments and advice from the likes of me. One of his favorite proverbs is "where you heart wants to go, your legs will take you." And when it comes to illustrations, he practices this philosophy. A marvelous man!

Again, I appreciate your consideration in Nairobi. Aniceti is extremely fortunate to have found 'patrons' like yourself and John Allen.

Best wishes, Sincerely, GWH

21 November 1971 Kitereza to Larson

Dear Miss Emilie Larson!

I am writing this letter to you because I wish to know how you are because I have not heard from you for some time. Why are you silent? Please contact Mrs. Shoonie Hartwig so that she can send me an answer quickly.

Since you sent me medicine for my cough, I have written two letters to thank you. Also, I received a letter from Mrs. Shoonie that they are now in a house with room for their four children and guests. But I am very sad because I have not heard from you after two letters. With this third letter, I beg you, please, send me an answer.

Perhaps you do not have someone near you to translate my letter. Has Bwana France returned to Nairobi?

About my book, Myombekere na Bugonoka, Mr. Markham in Nairobi at Heinemanns is considering it. He sent Mr. John Allen a copy of my manuscript who will help with the translation to English. Mr. Allen and his wife, Winnifred, came here and stayed two days – September 28/19 September 1971.

Mrs. Kitereza sends greetings! AK

---

25 November 1971 Markham to Hartwig

Dear Mr. Hartwig:

Aniceti Kitereza: BW. MYOMBEKERE and BI. BUGONOKA

Thank you for your letter of 1st November which accompanied your letter of the same date to the Editor of TRIBUS.

Thank you also for your handwritten letter of 15th November which accompanied a copy of a reply from Stuttgart.

I note that you are awaiting a decision from me concerning illustrations from TRIBUS for use in Aniceti's book, and I further note that only three figures in the TRIBUS article are the property of Stuttgart.

In due course I will let you know which other figures we propose to use and will then accept your offer of establishing from the two other Museums the question of reproduction rights.

Many thanks for your wishes.
Yours sincerely,

R.C. Markham cc: John Allen

1972

The letters of 1972 continue the collective quest to publish *Myombekere*. At the center of letter exchanges is Kitereza whose world now centers on hopeful waiting – not only for news of his book but the continuing assistance from Emilie Larson's commitment to his health and well-being. Just as his body is ailing, his spirit shows lack of confidence in those who say they are committed to his novel, but are they? Is there deceit among them? Why is it taking so long? Remember that he completed *Myombekere* in 1945. Waiting on the island in Lake Victoria is another world experience of isolation and time measured by how long it takes to walk from one place to another. Life on Ukerewe is in stark contrast to the bustling worlds of Nairobi, Arusha, London, Boston and Durham.

---

10 JANUARY 1972 KITEREZA TO LARSON

I have received your letter of November 15, 1971 that arrived December 9, 1971.

Before I reply to all matters, I would like to tell you that Father Deschamps, a priest in our Kagunguli Parish, friend of Mr. Hartwig and his wife Shoonie, arrived here in my house before your letter of November 15, 1971. Fr Deschamps came to see me in the morning of November 29, 1971, bringing with him a packet of medicine called "mylanta".100 tablets. It cost him $1 to get it out of the post office.

Fr Deschamps also asked me if you had written to say that you wrote me during the month of July 30, 1971???? Including $60.00. When he asked me I told him that I had not received such a letter from Miss Emilie Larson.

During that day I was greatly surprised, me a poor man, to fail to receive the gift you had written me in my poverty with my wife Anna Katura.

Also, on your side, I see you have incurred a great loss, my friend. Loo! Also Fr Deschamps continued to tell me that he had one cheque of $30.00 for me and he said that he would go to Mwanza to collect the money before Christmas. But, alas, up to now I have not seen him, even that money of the cheque I do not know anything!!

You, too, Miss Larson, said that in the late December 1971 that you would send me more money and more medicine! The month of December has gone by while I had fever and with great hopes and expectations that I would receive the things you said you would send me, but I have not received your letter in any of these things! I do not know what kept you busy, Miss Larson?

A friend of Dr. Jerry, Mr. Stanlake Samkange, gave you a telephone call telling you that he is from Rhodesia and has an American wife. He teaches at Harvard and his book has been published in the African Writer's Series!

Give my kind regards to all your relatives, especially David, his parents and sister. The blessing of God for the new year be yours and ours.

Mr. and Mrs. Aniceti Kitereza Ukerewe

---

21 FEBRUARY 1972 HARTWIG TO MARKHAM

Dear Mr. Markham,

I have been negligent on a matter that Aniceti Kitereza requested of me some weeks ago. He asked that a "synopsis" of the novel – Myombekere and Buganoka – that he prepared for us be forwarded to you. I wanted to check with you to determine if you in fact desired it. It was not quite the synopsis we had hoped for, more of a summary of the first chapters, but my wife was able to extract some excellent information from it that was included in the background article forwarded to you some months ago.

The material is in an exercise book and his comments are dispersed over 138 pages Hence, if you wish to see it, I will gladly post it by air.

I would also appreciate some indication from you regarding your impressions of the translated material. Is it too early to make a publication decision? We in the teaching profession are very much in need of a novel that is totally concerned with pre-colonial African society. I sincerely wish that Kitereza's work helps to fill this void.

I am looking forward to hearing from you. Sincerely,

Gerald Hartwig

2 MARCH 1972 KITEREZA TO LARSON

Dear Miss Larson!

Before I reply to the many parts of your 2 January letter, I must thank you for you continue to help me, you have not given up. The medicine you send for my rheumatism and my sustenance is cause for thanksgiving. May you know many blessings for I have not died yet!

On 24 February 1972 Father Deschamps brought me two checks – one for $30 and another for $20. It's important that you write on the check: Commercial Bank of Mwanza so that Father Deschamps doesn't have difficulty cashing it. This is so much money. Thank you!

I must tell you that a new hospital has just been opened. I will be able to get all the medicines that you have sent me which means that you no longer need to do so. If you continue sending money as you have to the fathers, then they can buy for me.

Mr. Hartwig has yet to hear about publishing. Mr. John Allen and his wife Winnifred tell me that the translation is now 124 pages. Your obedient friend, A. Kitereza

4 MARCH 1972 KITEREZA TO HARTWIG

Dr. Hartwig!

Since my last letter to you, 14 January, I have had no news from you since. You have work at your university which may be why the silence. I wait for news from Mr. Markham and Heinemanns!

Here, my wife and I continue to suffer with rheumatism so that I am not able to walk at all. In Emilie Larson's letter of 2 January 1972, she wrote me to say, "The Hartwigs are thrilled beyond words by news of John Allen's support of my work as well as his wife, Winnifred. They know that their translation cannot do justice to the author's work; Mr. Allen's work should be a fine piece."

These words surprised me greatly and my wife and I need to know what's behind these words! I cannot judge Mr. and Mrs. Allen's work. Mind you, they are now old; Allen is 68 years and Mrs. Winnifred is 70. My wife and I need to know what road we are on with MYOMBEKERE and BUGONOKA. You, Jerry, are the expert regarding books. We believe you must open your eyes regarding these people.

Since their visit here 30 September 1971, I have received two letters saying he has completed 60 pages in five months. Loo!! The first letter of 26 October 1971, Allen said he started the translation of Myombekere and made four copies, one to me, Markham and you and that we would see if it is good.

The second letter of 16 February 1972 I received after five months. Mrs. Winnifred wrote that they have had much work and can proceed with the translation a little at a time. Really, Dr. Jerry, this is taking a very long time – they now completed 124 pages.

I recall that Part I of Myombekere has about 400 pages and Part two about 400 with a total of 800. When will this be done? In what year?

I sent you the very complimentary words (from Allen) but I fear the words hide something else that is not good. Please, my friend, find out if this is good or bad.

Miss Larson also wrote me: "The best news of 1972 for the Hartwigs and me, will be news of your manuscript at Heinemanns."

I send you greetings also from my wife to you and all your family. Do you have snow in Durham? Mr. and Mrs. Kitereza

---

4 MARCH 1972 MARKHAM TO HARTWIG

Aniceti Kitereza: BW. MYOMBEKERE NA BI. BUGONOKA

Thank you for your letter of 21st February. I have delayed replying because of a business safari.

You mention Aniceti's "synopsis" of the novel which he sent you on 138 pages of an exercise book. I doubt if it would help me as I have seen the first chapters from which he obviously drew up his synopsis, but thanks for offering to it here.

Work on the project is extremely slow and I hasten to add that this is no fault of John Allen who translates on to tape for us to make into typescript. The enormous quantity of work put out by the small and devoted staff in this office has given us little time to look at Aniceti's novel. John's tapes are piling up awaiting transcription. He has done marvels and so has my secretary (who, incidentally, did NOT type this letter – the errors are mine!) but we find ourselves bogged down.

However, a young editor from my London office joins me next month for two years and in this time he will take on and train a Kenyan, so I am certain that soon we can give more time to Aniceti.

If is far too early to make a publishing decision. I must see more of the translated material. I appreciate your concern but I must be certain of this. John Allen is doing this work for nothing on his own tape recorder using his own tapes. I am apprehensive over the length of this book and having read the first few chapters, I feel we must do some drastic editing.

John is against this and feels it cannot and should not be edited down. He has suggested a double volume but I have doubts of the economics of such a scheme and naturally of the marketing.

I will keep in touch with you and write as soon as possible. I ought to warn you that I am taking two months leave in the U.K. from mid-April to mid-June but this should not interfere with the processing.

Yours sincerely, R.C.Markham cc: John Allen

---

10 MARCH 1972 HARTWIG TO MARKHAM

Dear Mr. Markham,

Thank you for your letter of March 4th explaining the situation in your office in relation to the Allen tapes of Kitereza's BW MYOMBEKERE NA BI BUGONOKA. If there is anything I can do, please let me know. I suppose I anticipate the arrival of your assistant about as much as you.

Your information is greatly appreciated. Sincerely,
GWH

cc. John Allen

---

18 MARCH 1972 ALLEN TO HARTWIG

Dear Dr. Hartwig:

Thank you very much for your letter to Bob Markham and for the note to me on it. Virtually all delay in Aniceti's work must be attributed to me. Shortage of staff may occasionally hold up the work at Bob's end; but he can do nothing until I supply the draft. This depends on how much time I can find. By editing Bob means cutting or abridging and to this I should not agree without severe pressure. I should prefer to shelve this problem until we have a clearer estimate of the length of the whole. At the moment it looks like 500/600 pp; but I have not done enough to be sure.

I think that some abbreviation could be made by transferring Aniceti's explanations of technical terms to notes or Appendices, where they could appear once, instead of, as it seems, several times. Whether this would make an appreciable difference I cannot yet tell. I cannot do this as I go along; it must wait until I can study a large bit of typescript. Similarly the book does fall naturally into two equal halves, so to make two books of it is not difficult; but we must make sure of the length before we think of this.

There are two ways in which we might be able to use financial help if you could find some and we should be most grateful. The obvious one would be to produce the whole work, subsidizing the price so that it costs no more than with Bob's proposed cuts. This we cannot consider yet. The other would be to speed things up and reduce Bob's initial costs. If I could find an adequate typist here, as is possible, it would ease the strain on Bob's staff and save me a great deal of trouble. This saving would be transferred to going on faster.

The present plan is that a) I do a tape, b) send it to Bob, who c) types it and returns three copies to me. I d) correct and e) send two copies to Aniceti who f) corrects and sends one copy back to me. I h) correct and i) send on copy to Bob, who j) corrects the fair copy and k) makes such retyping as is then necessary.

If I could find a typist, you will see that a great deal of delay would be cut out. I suggest that you ask Bob to make an extra copy of part of the original typescript and to let you have a substantial chunk of it. This will enable you to see more clearly what out difficulties are.

Yours sincerely, John Allen

---

21 March 1972 Hartwig to Kitereza (handwritten)

Dear Aniceti.

Greetings to you and your marvelous wife. The Hartwig family is in good health and good spirits. We received your letter yesterday in which you stated your concern about the novel. So let me tell you what I know.

I wrote to Mr. Markham on 21 February asking for information since 25 November was my last letter from him. His reply is what I had feared. Little is being done in Nairobi. Mr. Markham has received some tapes with translation from John Allen but they are not being transcribed, that is, typing Allen's translation. This is because of a shortage in clerical help. Mr. Markham sees no improvement until August or September when two more people join their staff. Although Mr. Allen is slow, he is doing better than the people in Nairobi.

However, it is important to remember that both Mr. Markham and Mr. Allen are doing this extra work because, at least Mr. Allen, they want your novel to be published – it is excellent literature.

For legal purposes, Mr. Allen will receive money for his translation work – he may have explained this to you – because when it is published his name will be mentioned as the translator. His fee will be 1/ Tshilling!! The typing in Nairobi is being done by the regular clerks after they finish their regular work, and they are very busy now so nothing is being done.

Mr. Markham is doing it this way to save money, otherwise he could take money from the sale of the book. I like his way of saving money but I am upset about the delay.

Furthermore, Mr. Markham is still concerned about the length of the book, even in English. As yet he has made no decision to publish the novel since he has not read it. I wrote Mr. Allen on March 10th asking if there was some way to speed up the process. To date I have received no reply. The most important man in this business at this time is Mr. Allen. So long as he is convinced that it should be published, it will be one way or another, whether it is Heinemann's or some other firm is not so important.

May I make a suggestion to you? Would it be possible for you to begin writing again? What to write about would be up to you and whether it would be a story or a longer work is again your decision. But with your knowledge about change during your own lifetime, you could make another excellent contribution. Please write and tell me if you are interested in what you would like to do. I have some ideas, too.

Sincerely, Jerry

---

17 APRIL 1972 KITEREZA TO HARTWIG

Thank you very much, Jerry, as your letter of 21 March 1972 arrived 30 March. I read that your family is all well as well as your heart!

Really, Dr. Hartwig, before I say more about our discussion, today you have encouraged me greatly and that you answered me so quickly, writing in your own hand. My friend, it is many days since you have hand written a letter, perhaps you have little time given your work at Duke University.

You have done a fine thing to write me by hand for you have taken away my concerns and doubts concerning Mr. R.C. Markham of Nairobi and Mr. John Allen of Arusha.

Your letter has helped me understand this journey. On 16 March 1972 I received 2 copies of the English translation that Mr. Markham in Nairobi sent to Father Deschamps in Nansio Ukerewe who then brought me the copies.

I have read Mr. Markham's letter asking me to make corrections and to send Registered Post to John Allen. I have finished this and on 1 April 1972, I sent a copy to Mr. Allen and kept one for myself. He has done a good job.

Mr. Allen wrote that he will be on safari for two months to Europe and unable to continue translating there until he returns in July 1972. Mrs. Allen wrote, "Myombekere na Bugonoka" is good! These days I wait and wait for letters from these men.

Also, Mr. Markham asked me to write a Preface but I wrote him that you had asked me for a synopsis so please send it to him. In this I have written an outline so please send that to them.

On another matter, you asked me to consider writing more about my life paying attention to what has changed. I will answer you.

Greetings to Mama of your children Shoonie! Let us thank God for his blessings!

Your faithful friend, AK

---

19 APRIL 1972 KITEREZA TO LARSON

Dear Miss Larson:

This year 1972 isn't the best one – it has not been raining yet. From December – even January through April, it didn't. So my dear, this old man realizes that during this year 1972, he will starve because we don't know where to escape to in order to cultivate or to be saved from this hunger. Me, poor and sick with rheumatism – if I could walk…I don't know where to run with my wife who has a heart disease.

It's humiliating to let you know about what I have seen – men who were dying from hunger 54 years ago. In 1919 when the war between England and Germany took place in Europe, I was a student in a German school. At that time, Tanzania was called German Colony – 'Deutsch-ost-Africa'. When the 1914-18 war broke out, Hitler sent a terrible message to all men of the German Colonies for help. So men were obliged to go in accordance with the message. Most of them who were taken from Ukerewe died during that war or were shot by the German Army. But the war drew to an end. Ukerewe men were discouraged to cultivate. Afterwards at the end of this war, influenza, cough and dysentery followed.

In 1919, all the countrymen were running short of food because they hadn't got food in reserve. Then they began taking by force or stealing grain from wealthy people. Many people during that disaster starved and were killing one another by weapons such as arrows. Finally the German Army brought us food from their country and we were saved. But we were emaciated, thin like a skeleton and tried to eat ripe fruit prematurely. My dear Larson, it was terrible and that's why I've wanted to let you know the calamity of hunger that 1972 is bringing us.

Your letter written on January 2 was received on Jan 16 and I answered you on March

2. Thank you. I've received your gift. Nowadays here, it's very hot day and night. We're sunburned and in a great sweat (because of living near the equator). It's out of the question to use a blanket. Peace to your sister, David and his sister. Happy Easter Day.

Well, I received on March 16 two copies of the translation of my book, 'Myombekere na Buganoka' from R.C. Markham P.O. Box 25080 Nairobi, Kenya East Africa and it was translated by J. Allen P.O. Box 254 Arusha, Tanzania; they sent them to us to correct and sign. One copy is for them. Another is mine. Surely Mr. Allen knows well how to translate accordingly just as I expected it to be. Mrs. Allen says it'll be a good book. Mr. J. Allen will go to Europe for two months and will be back the end of July.

I don't· know if my letter of thanks has arrived. Please let me know because I may forget.

Sincerely yours,

Mr. and Mrs. Aniceti Kitereza

---

12 MAY 1972 KITEREZA TO LARSON

Dear Emiie:

Thank you very much. Your letter of March 29 was received on April 23. On April 20, Fr. Deschamps brought me $20 and $5; he informed me that it was for buying medicine in Mwanza. I give you thanks for your generosity to me. I must answer your letter because of your concerns. Don't worry. About Fr Deschamps, he is a good-natured and honest man which is why I trust him. He is accustomed to bringing me money from you. I was upset when Fr Deschamps came and told me that did send me $60 but I told him that I hadn't received it. But now we have a better way of sending money and let me know when you send it.

I understand that you called Jerry and Shoonie on the telephone about my concerns regarding the time it is taking for Allen to translate and Markham to publish my book but now I understand better.

Now I believe that you have snow so that it is very cold. I am happy to hear that you are helping the one who translates my letter, Sam Killim to get a job. He knows old and new Swahili as well as French and English and he wishes to study. I think he'll make the best of it.

My dear, I don't forget to pray God to bless you in all you do. I give thanks to God for all your help because the rheumatism is still with me. God bless you.

Yours very truly,

Mr. and Mrs. Kitereza

---

9 August 1972 Kitereza to Larson

Dear Miss Emilie Larson!

Your letter of 22 July '72 has reached me on the 3rd of August as Fr Deschamps brought it with the $25 for which I thank you! Do not be concerned, my generous friend, all is well. Every day we give thanks to God for giving you a long life and to bless you in all you do, especially for us here in my home.

I was pleased to hear that your school is now closed giving you time to be with friends and family and Mama Shoonie. You will be in Minnesota to visit your aunts in August.

The medicine you sent me for diarrhea I finished quickly – what a pity! Perhaps you could send me more so that I have a back up. My wife and I continue to suffer. It is not possible for me to work in my farm, so I ask you for your continuing help. We are now old, my wife is 68 and I am 76. In addition, we have no family here to help us.

We are grateful that Fr Deschamps brings us the Ben Gay because there is none available here. He continues to help us!

Mr. John Allen in Arusha continues to translate my book into English. He wrote to say that he will come here to my house in October.

Mr. Samkange, a teacher and his wife you have met! And he now teaches at Harvard. He and Mr. Jerry became friends while they studied at Indiana University.

May you know God's many blessings and our thanks for your continuing blessings to us.

Mr. and Mrs. A. Kitereza

---

11 August 1972 Markham to Allen

Dear John:

BW. MYOMBEKERE NA BI. BUGONOKA

The first 33 pages of typescript were sent to Aniceti on 19th January. They were held up in Nansio P.O. and collected by Fr. Deschamps in mid-March.

These were sent in duplicate and he was asked to correct both, retain one and send on to you.

I can find nothing on file that he ever did send it to you. Please advise.

We are now approaching the stage of final decision-making and would like to see the 33 pages corrected by him and by you, for assessment. Please send.

In Dr. Gerald Hartwig's letter to me of 21st February he mentioned a "synopsis" of the novel prepared by Aniceti consisting of 138 pages corrected by him and by you, for assessment. Please send.

In Dr. Gerald Hartwig's letter to me of 21st February he mentioned a "synopsis" of the novel prepared by Aniceti consisting of 138 pages is in an exercise book. Dr. Hartwig said he would gladly post it to us by airmail. Would he now do so please?

If you have time, we would like you to give us an outline of the whole MS, showing:

1. *Chapters*
2. *A very brief 2 or 3-line description of what is in each chapter.*
3. *Likely overall length of typescript based on 9 foolscap double-spaced pages to a small tape, one side. (33 such pages represented four sides of 2 small, one side (33 such pages represented four sides of 2 small tapes).*
4. *General scope and development of the MS.*

Should you baulk at 3 above, we can work it out from the un-typed tapes in our possession.

As we have lost Brenda (our typist who typed the first 33 pages from tae), we just go to a local Secretarial College for help with the rest. We have 3 ½ small tapes and 6 large tapes, double-sided, which you have prepared and which need transferring on to type. One college has quoted Shs. 8/ per page which works out an a114 pound outlay. We have to decide if we can afford this. Hence this letter.

Could you work on the above, please, John. Yours sincerely,

R.C. Markham

cc: Mr. Aniceti Kitereza Dr. Gerald Hartwig USA

---

16 August Kitereza to Hartwig

Dear J. Hartwig!

Thank you for your letter of July 12 which I received July 25. Inside the packet you sent the article you wrote for AFRICAN HISTORICAL STUDIES Vol.

IV No. 3 1971. It was exciting to read about my relatives who were chiefs. I really thank you for your hard work writing our history.

In your letter you wrote that you are traveling with Shoonie and the children to Colorado and Minnesota and that it is 4,350 miles. Will you fly or go by car? Also you wrote that these days the weather is hot. I am happy to hear there is no snow. And you also wrote about your writing. Your title THE ART OF SURVIVAL is excellent. Your writing is so good. Keep on, bwana!! Also, I read ihat you name me as an informant. I thank you very much.

You also wrote about Fr Henryk-Zimon who has written about the Kerebe in German. I have yet to see it, and I would very much like a copy. It is three years since he was here and now I think he is in Switzerland or Poland.

You told me also that Christopher, Karl, Kari and Kurt Gerald are growing and are very excited about vacation and your safari. Here, we are old and suffer with diseases from morning to night, my friend. Our house is like a hospital. Fr Deschamps brings us medicine and money from our friend Emilie Larson. We are so grateful for all she does for us and pray her life is as long as ours.

Concerning my book and Mr. Markham, he has not seen the translation yet and he's written Mr. Allen and me to send the Preface quickly as well as a negative picture of me to use in Myombekere. Also, Mr. Allen and his assistant will come to my home in October.

Now I wait for your response to two copies. Anna sends her greetings to your family. May god bless you and us, also.

Your friend, AK

---

24 AUGUST 1972 MARKHAM TO HARTWIG

Dear Dr. Hartwig:

Many thanks for your letter of 17th August and for the safe arrival of the Synopsis which we will look at and which should give us a very good idea regarding final publication.

I am rather touched by your offer to help with part of the expenses of publishing but I regret I cannot accept your offer as the outlay leading up to the publication of this book is our responsibility and one on which we would hope to make a profit.

Best wishes,

R.C. Markham

13 September 1972 Markham to Hartwig

Dear Dr. Hartwig:

BW. MYOMBEKERE and BI. BUGONOKA

John Allen suggested recently that we should try to get a subsidy for this book from an American source.

He translated into Swahili some time ago a study of the people of Lindi called WAKILINI and it was published by the East African Literature Bureau, Nairobi. I have just made a second edition.

It was subsidized by two American organizations: The African Studies Program of Boston University, and, The Aquinas Fund of New York. I have no addresses.

He offered to write to both organizations suggesting they subsidize Aniceti's book but I felt such an approach would come better from you and John agreed.

John states that his publishers were very gloomy over the possible sales of his Swahili book, hence demanded a subsidy before publication and obtained it. He is very optimistic about sales of Aniceti's book so suggests that any subsidy could take the form of a guarantee sooner than a cash advance. He quotes other publishers as asking for a promise to pay for unsold stock of x copies after y years and that if the publisher did not call on the donor, it is therefore available for a similar book.

I would not quibble over this approach but I would be happier with a cash advance as we have spent so much time (not much money) on it. As you know, our time is money as we are prevented working on other books.

I feel you know as much about the history of this book as anybody so could paint a true picture. For the record, John Allen translates Aniceti's Swahili on to tape into English. We put his tape on to typescript. Our expert who started the job has left us and you know I am thinking of putting it out to a local Secretarial Bureau. John has completed 12 tapes double-sided of which 2 ½ are on typescript.

Originally we were quite happy with the typescript as typed from tape but I have had a closer look and decided that it badly and drastically needs corrections, alterations, additions and deletions. I have been doing this work over the past week or two. We must therefore change our method of work. Whoever types the script must type one draft copy only. This will be edited and it will then be typed in triplicate. The other way was a waste of paper and of John Allen's and Aniceti's time.

John Allen and his wife plan to visit Aniceti again very shortly and stay with Father Deschamps for a few days. He therefore wants to take to Aniceti as much of his translated work as possible. I am working at this like mad to please John and to placate Aniceti. All the original pages have been re-typed and I am working on more tapes, slowly but conscientiously and John should be able to show Aniceti that we have not completely bogged down.

Please let me know what you think of the idea of a subsidy and if you are prepared to make the first approach. Please realize that if you prefer not to enter into this I will fully understand and will not hold it against you.

Yours sincerely,

R.C. Markham
cc: John Allen

---

20 SEPTEMBER 1972 HARTWIG TO MARKHAM HAND- WRITTEN

Dear Mr. Markham

I shall initiate efforts here to locate a source that will subsidize Aniceti's book. The following questions come to mind that will hopefully aid me in this task:

1) *amount of subsidy for the English edition?*
2) *amount of subsidy for a Swahili version?*
3) *are both sections (part 1 and 2) involved or only one?*

Am I correct in assuming that with a subsidy you will proceed with the printing?

I'll start immediately to search on this end although nothing formal can be done until some estimates are in hand.

Sincerely, G Hartwig

---

22 SEPTEMBER 1972 HARTWIG TO TAYLOR (DUKE POLITICAL SCIENCE) HANDWRITTEN

Dear Taylor:

I've enclosed a portion of the relevant correspondence that has accumulated over the past 20 months concerning the manuscript I referred to last Monday. On the basis of John Allen's assessment and his willingness to translate the 850 manuscript pages into English, I am convinced of the merits within the work itself. If not it appears only a subsidy is lacking – it has taken considerable time to even reach this stage!

This week I requested Markham to provide a specific amount necessary for publication. The amount will vary depending upon whether both parts are published and whether Swahili version is also considered.

A thought came to mind today which may be totally out of the question but would this be an opportunity for students interested in African culture to become involved? That is, to establish a fund specifically for this purpose and encourage them to see it through.

I'm not familiar with the Aquinas Fund and I know the program at Boston is hard pressed financially. Is Shell a possibility with their East African interests?

Jerry

September 1972 Taylor to Hartwig

Dear Jerry:

I do not at the moment have any helpful suggestions as to success for a subsidy. The Shell Foundation would hardly be interested. I am doubtful if our own limited funds should be used for "outside" purposes. However, I shall give the matter some thought and pass on any ideas that come to me. Taylor

---

26 September 1972 Markham to Hartwig

Dear Dr. Hartwig

Thank you for your letter of 20th September and thanks too for offering to try for a subsidy for Aniceti's book.

It seems obvious to me that the English edition is 'made' for inclusion in the African Writers Series, all titles of which are published in London because of their international appeal. However, my London office may also agree and it would then be left to my office to publish.

I must have sufficient pages of the typescript collected here, edited by Aniceti and by John Allen, then professionally edited by us, before asking London to consider its inclusion in the A.W.S. London would want to see this typescript and the longer it is the better.

If London accepted it for inclusion in the A.W.S. there would be no great need for a subsidy (though they are always welcome) as the series sells as a series So, I think therefore that your approach for a subsidy for the English edition should be based on the assumption that it will be published in East Africa with a proviso that London may wish to to take it.

Of such a book we would probably want to print 3000 copies originally. I estimate the cost to us as Shs. 6/- per copy which includes all production costs but which excludes our own time and royalties. If we could interest an American publisher in purchasing an edition or a quantity, this unit cost could be reduced.

It has always appeared to me that the use of both parts I and II of Aniceti's MS would make too large a single volume unless it was drastically edited and reduced. Marketing two volumes would be a hazard and I would be against it. So the answer is to reduce his two parts to a single volume. Having been engaged in this work on Aniceti recently, I realize there is much repetition and the book can be cut down without losing its natural punch.

The Swahili version is an unknown. Aniceti's Swahili MS is far too long for pubication and I am as much against a 2-volume edition of a Swahili book as an English book.

John Allen has a colleague in mind who would be prepared to re-write or re-frame the MS but he would have to be very firmly briefed to reduce it in size In fact, it might be easier in the long run to translate back into Swahili the results of the edited English version, even though the idea sounds crazy.

With this in mind, I would guess that the Swahili edition would cost more than the English edition. We would print again 3000 copies and I estimate the unit cost at Shs. 8/- which includes outside translation or editorial help but again which excludes our own time and royalties. If we could interest a Tanzanian publisher in purchasing an edition or quantity thus unit cost could be reduced.

The above I think has answered your three leading questions. If we are successful with a generous subsidy we would definitely publish and the English edition would be published first.

I would like to stress, even though you know it, that John Allen is doing all his work on this for practically nothing and that his thought, time and labour are not costed into the above estimates.

Good luck.

As soon as I have enough of a sizeable beginning to a typescript, I will post a copy to you, s that you can see what has been done.

Yours sincerely,

R.C. Markham
cc: John Allen

10 OCTOBER 1972 HARTWIG TO LARSON HANDWRITTEN

Dear Emily,

The enclosed is apparently as specific as Markham is going to be.

I intend to check here in Durham with North Carolina Mutual Insurance Co., a large Black owned company to see if they have any interest in the arts.

Oh me!
Cheers,
Jerry

19 OCTOBER 1972 HERDECK TO HARTWIGS – GERALD/CHARLOTTE (HERDECK, SENIOR EDITOR BLACK ORPHEUS PRESS, WASHINGTON, D.C.)

Dear Research Persons:

I am preparing a bio-bibliographic study of 350 African authors and should much appreciate the opportunity of using the photograph, or having your permission to reproduce it, of Aniceti Kitereza, the Kerebe Novelist, which appeared in the 2nd number, Vol. 3 of RESEARCH IN AFRICAN LITERATURES. I shall of course give the usual credits and will be happy to pay for postage and the cost of a glossy print, or I could return the positive to you in a month or so. I shall need the photo within the next two weeks to meet my deadline.

May I say I enjoyed your article very much and have made a brief entry for Kitereza who appears to deserve recognition very much. Could you tell us whether the English translation and publication of novel from Swahili has advanced beyond the stage mentioned in your article?

Sincerely,

Donald E. Herdeck

31 OCTOBER 1972 HARTWIG TO HERDECK

Dear Mr. Herdeck:

Thank you for your inquiry concerning Aniceti Kitereza of October 19th. Enclosed is the print of Kitereza that appeared in RESEARCH IN AFRICAN LITERATURES.

Progress in the realm of publication, this has been a rather long ordeal in itself. As it now stands Mr. R. C. Markham of Heinemann's in Nairobi has agreed to publish an English edition if I can provide a subsidy. An additional subsidy will be necessary for a Swahili edition.

I understand Markham's problem because the manuscript's nature entails unusual costs. It is being translated from Swahili now by John Allen who is living in Arusha, Tanzania, and who originally (as a reader) encouraged Henemann's to publish it. Allen has visited Kitereza twice to discuss the translation. Allen is sufficiently sold on the value of the manuscript and respects the author to the degree that he is undertaking the translation for a fee of one shilling! However, he puts the translation on tape and then sends it to Nairobi for transcription and editing. It is in these latter processes that the expenses are encountered.

In brief, that is the way things stand at the present time. If you have any suggestions, I would certainly appreciate hearing from you. Markham is also interested in finding an American publisher to assist in the volume's dissemination.

Sincerely yours,
GWH

---

2 November 1972 Markham to Hartwig

Dear Dr. Hartwig: BWANA MYOMBEKERE AND BIBI BUGONOKA

Many thanks for your letter of 27 October in which you asked me to write you an "official" letter in which I cite all our unusual expenses in producing the above book and the estimated extra costs entailed.

You ask for this "official" letter because you wish to make use of it in your application to various bodies asking them if they are interested in a subsidy.

There is one untruth in the "official" letter as John Allen will not ask for a fee for his translation work as he has already stated, but I had to include it in the letter or people may have enquired why it was missing.

I feel that even though John Allen is not asking for a fee, we can always find use for the 250 pounds mentioned in other spheres of editorial work.

I note from your letter that you have already approached the North Carolina Mutual Life Insurance Co. and although I appreciate your contact with these people I would ask if it is your intention to follow up on an earlier letter of mine in which I mentioned the two organizations which subsidized a Swahili book of John Allen's, namely, The African Studies Program of Boston University and The Aquinas Fund of New York. For your information, the synopsis which you sent to me some time ago and which was in Aniceti's hand writing contained a useful introduction to the book which John Allen has taped and which is now in typescript form. John Allen is grateful to you for studying the synopsis as it contains much information useful to him in his translation work.

Back to the subsidy, you ask me for a minimum necessary amount of subsidy I have in mind in case you have to negotiate with any organization and I feel that $1,000 would be a minimum whereas the maximum is completely up to you.

I trust that I have enthused sufficiently in the "official" letter but if you feel that I haven't and that you need something different, would you please let me know and I will alter or add to the letter.

With best wishes.

Yours sincerely,

R. C. Markham
cc: John Allen

---

5 NOVEMBER 1972 ALLEN TO HARTWIG

Dear Dr. Hartwig: BWANA MYOMBEKERE AND BIBI BUGONOKA

I think it is time for you and me to get together and in any case I have promised to send you Aniceti's warm greetings. This year we found him older; but still hearty and keen. We are most anxious to get on as fast as possible; but there are one or two points in Markham's letters of 2 Nov that need a bit of clarification.

Translator's fee. I have had trouble in the past and want my position to be absolutely clear to Aniceti and others. I do not want to make money out of him, so I suggested to Markham that I have a fee of one shilling written into the contract so that there be no feeling that I have made something somewhere on the side. But if this only means that I am saving money for the printer or the publisher or reducing the price of the book by a minute amount (and therefore Aniceti's percentage) I should prefer to have the $250 and make it over to him.

It is true that I was asked to reduce the length and that I tried to do so; but not at the cost of omitting valuable material or spoiling the style. Hence I have only reduced very slightly indeed, cutting out repetitious explanations and (with Aniceti's approval) putting these into a glossary. The book then remains too long for a single volume and Markham has capitulated and will make two vols of it. It falls naturally into two parts and I am sure that this is the right course.

The Swahili: Aniceti's translation from Kerebe to Swahili was done in haste. He frequently leaves out a word or a syllable and makes many spelling errors. I do not want to change the style at all; but corrections are necessary and I know no one but myself who would take the trouble to make them. After this it would have to be retyped. I think the best course would be to have a second photo- copy made of the ms and I work on this for the typist. This I cannot attempt at present. Keen though I am, I have a job to do and I am committed to three other bits of editing and translation, which have to take priority. One is almost finished and I shall do it in Dec. One I am doing now and hope to finish before I go to Nairobi in Dec. The third will take some 50 hrs and when I make them I do not know. Then I shall return to the translation. I have taped 550 pp out of some 900, so we are getting on. Part I is complete and half typed.

I hope that the popularity of the English Edition will lead to a demand for the Swahili Edition. That will have to wait; but I do hope to do it.

Incidentally, I am much interested in your photo copy. Could you let me know its name? None of us know of a machine which will do both sides of the paper.

I should like to thank you for rescuing Aniceti's work. You will never regret doing so.

Yours sincerely,

John Allen

---

26 November 1972 Herdeck to Hartwig Dear

Dr. Hartwig:

Thank you indeed for the quick response to my request for a photo of Aniceti Kitereza. I appreciated learning about the difficulties encountered by John Allen and others in preparing the ms for Heinemann's. I can promise nothing at this time but I am scouting for manuscripts for the new firm of Black Orpheus which is bringing out my own bio-bibliographic volume of African writing and possibly, if we could see some pages 2 to 30) of the English translation, there might be something to be said.

Heinemann's is now considering bringing out one of our books in its African Writers series, Rene Maran's BATOUALA, and has expressed an interest in mine. Possibly, if Heinemann's does go forward we might think of doing the American edition.

Do you think it would be useful at this time to get in touch with R.C. Markham in Nairobi? I can get the address but if you have it, I would appreciate learning what you suggest, for the Kitereza story as "story", is interesting and just possibly a fine piece of writing might be before us.

Again, thank you for your quick response to my letter. I shall return the photo as soon as possible (it's now being prepared for the cut).

Sincerely,

Donald E. Herdeck

---

16 NOVEMBER 1972 KITEREZA TO LARSON

Dear Emilie Larson!

Your letter of 19 October '72 I received on 4 November '72. Mr. John Allen arrived here, his second visit, on 12 October '72. We talked about Mr. Markham in Nairobi who sent 50 pounds. It will come by check to Fr. Van der Wee who is now my agent as Fr Deschamps will return to Canada in December who is no longer able to hear well. So please note this change if you send me anything.

Because Mr. and Mrs. Allen were here three days, we talked about Kikerebe words that I use in my book that will be in a glossary. Mr. Jerry Hartwig, really, he is working hard to help me receive money for my writing.

Thank you Miss Emilie for your gifts which Fr Deschamps brought – a tube of Ben-Gay and $30. You have made our lives (me and my wife) so much better, I simply do not have words enough to say how grateful we are. You told me that David would write, but as yet I have not received it. Perhaps he has too much to do including the piano study. Please greet him and all of your family.

Mr. and Mrs. A. Kitereza

---

17 NOVEMBER 1972 KITEREZA TO HARTWIG

Dear Jerry!

Today I am thinking of you in my heart even though you are so many miles away. I hope this finds you and your family well! For me, not much has changed since you were here in 1968 and 1969. My rheumatism continues and because the rains began the first of November it is more of a problem.

Thank you for sending Volume IV of African Historical Studies. You have honored me – "Aniceti Kitereza: A Kerebe Novelist." Mrs. Kitereza said that you are not only a good man but kindly! And because of your efforts, I have received money for my writing.

Good news: Mr. John Allen told me that Mr. Markham sent a check of 50 pounds to Fr van der Wee who is replacing Fr Deschamps because he is returning to Canada.

My dear friend, greet all in your family.
Mr. and Mrs. Aniceti Kitereza

---

30 November 1972 Hartwig to Markham

Dear Mr. Markham:

Enclosed is a letter from Donald Herdeck of Black Orpheus Press. He saw the article about Kitereza in the latest issue of RESEARCH IN AFRICAN LITERATURES and enquired about it since he wanted to include Kitereza in his bio-bibliographic volume of African writers. I took the opportunity to inform him of the present need for a subsidy in addition to someone to distribute the publication in the U.S. I shall let you take it from this point, particularly the sending of 20-30 pages for him to see if this seems a reasonable route. I shall respond to his letter indicating that I have forwarded a copy of his letter to you.

I have also made an effort to solicit at least advice if not money from Francis X. Sutton who is still with the Ford Foundation in New York. According to unofficial sources he has a "soft spot" when it comes to East Africa. Your "official" letter was forwarded to him along with a couple of earlier missives to provide some background to Kitereza and the novel. I also requested a $2500 subsidy for a Swahili edition since $1500 is hardly worth the paper work at Ford. I am fairly optimistic about this attempt. One of our faculty members here at Duke works at the Foundation on a part-time basis and I intend to push him. He is the person who recommended Sutton in the first place.

I received a letter from Kitereza today indicating that John Allen had visited him in October. The 50 pound advance was also mentioned – marvelous! Incidentally, it was Father van der Wee who kept the final copy of the novel all these years in safe-keeping for Aniceti. The circle is virtually complete now; van der Wee was a friend of Simard's who employed Aniceti and encouraged him to write in the first place!

Best wishes,

Gerald Hartwig

2 November 1972 Markham to Hartwig

Dear Dr. Hartwig: BWANA MYOMBEKERE and BIBI BUGONOKA

By Aniceti Kitereza

As you are an "interested" party in the publication of the above book, having done research in the past in the Ukerewe Islands on southern Lake Victoria, Tanzania, the locale of this tale, I feel I should acquaint you with difficulties we are having before we can hope to have a manuscript in our hands for presentation to the printer.

The author spent several years writing the book which is in two parts. His original manuscript was handwritten in the Kiswahili language and it was offered to us for publication about 2 years ago.

Because of its length and its somewhat old-fashioned approach to written Swahili we rejected its publication but suggested we were very interested in an English edition. The author, who is an excellent linguist, does not command a good knowledge of English, so he could not rewrite it in English.

The matter was mentioned to a noted Swahili scholar, John Allen, who, after reading a few chapters of the Swahili MS offered to translate it into English. At our request he tried to reduce its length in his translation. His stipulation was that he would only translate on to tape and left it to us to transfer from tape to typescript.

We do not have the staff to cope with typing from tape recorder to script and have had to farm out the job to a local secretarial bureau at enormous expense. To date we are less than half way through the first part. The bureau charge K.Shs. 8/- per page of typescript and although we have managed to do about 68 pages ourselves, we cannot keep it up and the balance will have to be done outside. My estimation of the work of Part 1 of this book is 284 pages which works out at K.Shs. 2272/ or 114 Pounds. year and

John Allen has had cause to visit the author in Ukerewe Islands twice over the past year and we have had to foot his expenses. To date our expense bill is K.Shs. 2054 – 103 Pounds. I feel that he must undertake at least two more safaris which will mean a further 103 Pounds.

John Allen's fee for the translation has been left to us and as we have a good local reputation we have to offer him at least 250 Pounds for his extremely hard and devoted work. Our local editing fees would be included in the purchase price of the book if and when published. The author would receive a royalty on sales.

We are rather desperately seeking a subsidy for the publication of this book. Our outlay to date has been 217 Pounds and I anticipate a further outlay of 335 Pounds, making a total of 570 Pounds which in dollars is approximately $1500. This amount, of course, does not include printers bills, artists' charges, etc. as these will be borne by us when the production is in process.

Any help you can give us in shape of a subsidy would be very welcome. I know of your own interest in the author and his work and I hope you will be able to impress other people.

We, in Heinemann's, are very enthusiastic about Aniceti's book. It has an immediate appeal to all people interested in the culture of Africa. The author has a very sincere style and his story, brilliantly translated from the Swahili, is extremely interesting and gives, in novel form, the ways of the Ukerewe people before the coming of the white man. Until the manuscript is finalized, we cannot offer it to any professional reader, but those people who have seen it or heard it on tape are very enthusiastic and the publication of such a work is a must.

Please try to help. Yours sincerely,

R.C. Markham

---

28 November 1972 Hartwig to Sutton

Dear Dr. Sutton:

I requested Craufurd Goodwin for advice concerning a subsidy to publish a novel by a Tanzanian author. His immediate response was to redirect the inquiry to you, so here I am.

Enclosed are relevant bits of correspondence concerning the manuscript as well as a Xerox copy of an article on the author, Aniceti Kitereza, that was published this fall in RESEARCH IN AFRICAN LITERATURES. Briefly, let me fill you in on the background of the situation.

I conducted historical research on Bukerebe (Ukerewe) Island in the Tanzanian portion of Lake Victoria in 19768-69. During this period I met Kitereza and eventually learned of the existence of a Kikerebe manuscript that he had completed in 1945. One extant copy of this manuscript, a novel, remained in the possession of a Dutch priest who had been literally keeping it dry for Kitereza since the 1950s. Around 1950 Father Simard, Kitereza's employer, had corresponded with the East African Literature Bureau about publishing the text in Kikerebe. The limited readership in that language weighed against its publication. Since the work was aimed at Kerebe youngsters in primary schools no further effort was made to have the manuscript published, even in Swahili. Simard's death shortly thereafter mitigated against any further publication efforts.

Late in 1968 I took up where Simard left off. I convinced Kitereza, by now badly crippled by rheumatism, that if he wanted anything to come of his earlier efforts he would have to translate the manuscript into Swahili – which he completed. Fifteen months later I was then in possession of over 850 ledger pages of Swahili manuscript. It was subsequently duplicated and submitted to Heinemann's in Nairobi for consideration. Although a reader in Mwanza sat on the manuscript for 6 months, the response from the first reader, John Allen, was sufficiently enthusiastic to warrant serious consideration from R.C. Markham in Heinemann's Nairobi office.

Allen, in order to convince Markham of the value of the manuscript, started translating it onto tapes. For the past 12 months Allen has periodically worked on this endeavor since he had no assurance from Markham that it would be published. But as the copy of Markham's letter of November 2, 1972 indicates, an English version will be published providing a subsidy is found.

The unusual expenses arise from Kitereza's training. His education at the Bukoba seminary was completed in 1919 which means his Latin, German and French were well grounded but his limited English has come via a German-English dictionary since all the White Fathers conversed in French or German. Furthermore, his Swahili is of an earlier up-country vintage, and it is not desirable to publish it as it now stands. Hence the need for someone like Allen to do an English translation. The length of the novel – the original Kikerebe manuscript was 300 typed single-spaced pages in length also presents unusual problems. All in all, Allen has advised doing an English version first, since it will be marketable, and then worry about a Swahili version. Allen's agreement to do the translating was based on his need to put it on tape. The transcription and editing is where the extraordinary costs begin to emerge.

The contents of the novel make it unique for eastern Africa. Kitereza is of Kenyatta's generation, a well -educated man who never rose beyond the level of karani, a man who respected some western values and innovations, but who never disowned his cultural heritage. It was this respect for former values that stimulated Kitereza to write the novel in the first place. Children attending primary school in the early 1940s disdained the wisdom of their ancestors. Kitereza's novel was intended to reveal another world to these youngsters, one that existed before the Europeans arrived, one that should not be totally ignored. It is the novel's purpose and intended readership that makes it so valuable today to non-Kerebe readers, whether in this country or in Tanzania. Being a non-political writer of his particular generation makes it an exceptional contribution.

I have informed Mr. Markham that I would attempt to find a subsidy for the manuscript. While I am particularly keen as a teacher to use the English edition in my own classes, I think it would be inexcusable not to work toward a Swahili edition as well since it is East African literature. As Markham indicates in his letter, a subsidy of

$1500 is necessary for the English edition. A Swahili edition would require $2500 to insure a low cost edition for the East African market.

As we are all aware, acquiring financial support for the arts is not all that easy, whether now or even five years ago. I would certainly appreciate any suggestions you might have on this.

Sincerely,

Gerald W. Hartwig

---

1 December 1972 Hartwig to Herdeck

Dr. Mr. Herdeck:

Thank you for your letter of 26 November.

Concerning getting in touch with R.C. Markham in Nairobi, I have taken the liberty of Xeroxing your letter of the 26th and forwarding it to Markham today suggesting that he take the initiative at this stage, particularly when it comes to letting you examine some of the text. Arrangements between publishers are outside my experience but I would imagine a wait on your part of three weeks or so would not be out of line.

Markham who I've been corresponding with for two years now on this manuscript is prompt in his correspondence.

This much I do know. He would like to get the English version of the manuscript in order and then submit it to the London office for assessment for the African Writers Series. If they are not interested – there is a length problem yet to be resolved – he then intends to publish it in Nairobi. The important thing is that he has made the decision that it will be published. Consequently John Allen, who has only worked occasionally on the translation during the past 12 month, intends to complete his end of the work by working full time on it beginning in January.

Markham has also committed himself to the extent of a 50 Pound advance to Kitereza, a situation which I learned from Kitereza's letter that arrived this morning. If I'm not mistaken it is Allen's persuasiveness and insistence that is moving the show at this point. He visited Kitereza for the 3rd time October 12th – 15th to go over his translation. Kitereza's captivating personality as well as advanced age are factors that have contributed to the urgency of completing the task as soon as possible. An interesting but time-consuming project, this but terribly worthwhile.

Sincerely, Gerald Hartwig

---

7 December 1972 Markham to Herdeck

Dear Sir: BWANA MYOMBEKERE AND BIBI BUGONOKA

Your name has been given to me by Dr. Gerald Hartwig of Duke University and he has sent me a copy of your letter to him of November 26th.

You ask for 20-30 pages of Aniceti Kitereza's manuscript in English which at the moment bears the above title. You feel that there may be sufficient "meat" in these pages to give him a mention in your own bio-bibliographic volume on African writing and also to enable you to judge, possibly, if you would want to do the American edition.

These are early days yet because as you have been told by Dr. Hartwig, we do not know if the English edition is publishable and if it will be published by London or Nairobi. I have personally been connected with this book since the beginning and I am convinced it will be published but I am a cog in a larger wheel.

At the moment the manuscript is being put on to typescript in English from tape translated live from the Swahili by John Allen. The first part of Kitereza's massive work will fill one book the size of a normal volume in the African Writer's Series, and even then would have to be edited down more than somewhat. We are nearing the end of the first part and it is my intention to do the necessary editing over the Christmas holiday. I should be able to have 20-30 pages of edited work ready for you in early- January and I shall send them to you.

At this stage you should deal with me and not with my London office, publishers of the African Writers Series, as, until they have in their hands a complete manuscript of part I, they cannot possibly give an opinion on publication.

Yours faithfully,

R.C. Markham

Dr. Hartwig: many thanks for yours of November 30th and your welcome news of Herdeck's interest and what is better the possible interest of the Ford Foundation in a subsidy. Keep up the good work!

John Allen: for all our sakes, please stop taping any more of Part II. Even if you have time between your other projects please don't work on Aniceti, have a break. Let us see what happens to Part I.

cc: Dr. Gerald Hartwig, USA John Allen, Arusha

---

12 December 1972 Sutton (Ford Foundation) to Hartwig

Dear Professor Hartwig:

Thank you for your letter of November 28 regarding the possibility of support for the publication of Aniceti Kitereza's novel. We will have to check with our Nairobi office, and this will unfortunately involve some delay. But we would like to assure you that we will consider your request sympathetically.

Sincerely yours,

Francis X. Sutton
Deputy Vice President Ford Foundation

---

14 December 1972 Hartwig to Markham

Dear Mr. Markham:

This morning's mail brought the enclosed note from Francis Sutton of the Ford Foundation concerning Aniceti's novel. If I read this correctly, the ball is now in your court since the Ford people in Nairobi will undoubtedly check with you as well as John Allen. That Sutton did not immediately refuse to consider the small sum requested appears to me to be the most important hurdle. The value of the novel itself should convince them that it is a worthwhile endeavor. If I'm not mistaken the decision concerning support will be made in Nairobi, not New York. Good luck!

Sincerely,

Gerald Hartwig

20 December 1972 Markham to Hartwig

Dear Dr. Hartwig: BW. MYOMBEKERE AND BI. BUGONOKA

Thanks for your letter with enclosures.

I am naturally very pleased with your efforts with the Ford Foundation and will await their approach from their Nairobi Office.

John Allen is spending three weeks over Christmas in Nairobi and is working on the rest of the pages making up Part I. We should soon have an edited typescript.

Happy Christmas and again many thanks.

Yours sincerely,

R.C. Markham

1973

It is now four years since this publishing epic began. The number of letters exchanged during this time frame are a testament to the shared commitment between Hartwig, Markham, Allen, Larson, Catholic Fathers and Kitereza to bring MYOMBEKERE to life. As the number of letter exchanges begins to diminish, one could assume that epic fatigue has taken over. And what of Kitereza, who continues to live time slowly on Ukerewe, diligently writing blue aerograms? He is 77 years old and his body frailty increases. Yet within the letters written and received, hope persists.

---

8 January 1973 Markham to Herdeck

Dear Sir,

BWANA MYOMBEKERE AND BIBI BUKONOKA

Further to my letter of 7th December, I am sending to you under separate cover, the first 37 pages of the manuscript plus the author's introduction.

The former is just readable as it has been heavily corrected and I hope you will be able to get an opinion from it. The latter is uncorrected and will be edited down when we publish.

Will you please acknowledge receipt of these pages and in due course, let me know how you feel about an American edition.

Yours sincerely,

R.C. Markham

cc: Dr. Hartwig USA

Mr. John Allen Tanzania

---

8 JANUARY 1973 MARKHAM TO KITEREZA

Dear Aniceti:

BW. MYOMBEKERE AND BI. BUGONOKA

I have sent you under separate cover by registered airmail, the following items:

1. *John Allen's report giving progress on your book to the end of 1972.*
2. *Two copies of the typescript pages 122 to 255 which are sent to you for a final check.*
3. *Two copies of John Allen's suggested glossary.*
4. *Two copies of a page of queries which John Allen has raised and which refer to the pages of typescript no. 1 to 121.*

The first half of your manuscript which is now in type (pages 1 to 121) is now in my possession and is fully connected and ready for submission to my London office.

However, I will naturally wait until the second half of the manuscript (pages 122 to 255) have been returned to me from you and John Allen.

You know the routine so will you please follow it as previously. Yours sincerely,

R.C. Markham

cc. John Allen Arusha Dr. G. Hartwig, USA

---

15 JANUARY 1973 KITEREZA TO LARSON

Dear Miss Larson:

I received on Jan 7 1973 the letter you wrote on December 14 '72 that you sent by airmail including $20 through Fr van der Wee. Thank you very much for your gifts which console me every day. Many times we are looking at your picture taken by your nephew David. We are aware of how busy you are. In spite of that you're still remembering us. Again, we thank you!

The bank of this place now requires your checks to be sent to the Dar es Salaam Bank. What a pity!!! You say that it is a long time since you've heard from the Hartwigs in Durham but that Mama Shoonie is traveling with a group of singers. She must be a music expert.

I received the 50 Pound advance from Markham in Nairobi. It was sent through Fr van der Wee. On Mr. John Allen's second journey to my home, he saw Mr. Markham in Nairobi to settle the matter of the money. On Allen's return home, he saw Mr.

Markham again to report on his visit.

Since December '72, I have been very anemic and so my health continues to be a problem.

May God bless you and us! Aniceti Kitereza

---

5 FEBRUARY 1973 MARKHAM TO HERDECK

Dear Mr. Herdeck,

BWANA MYOMBEKERE AND BIBI BUGONOKA

Many thanks for your kind letter of January 16th. The delay in answering is due to my absence in Zambia and Malawi.

I must remind you of my words in an earlier letter that at this stage we do not know if the English edition is to be published in London or in Nairobi. You have therefore jumped the gun a little when you ask if we can come to some informal agreement at this stage.

If the book is published in London, and I sincerely hope it will be as this means an international publication and not merely a local book, then London must have the option of choosing an American publisher for an American edition. They know in London of Black Orpheus Press and I will mention your and their possible interest when the time is ripe. However, they have their own outlets and may wish to choose another publisher.

In your item 3, you ask who controls the rights. This of course depends who publishes it. Kitereza will have the copyright but we usually work on the author's behalf when chasing further sources of revenue. As I mentioned earlier, there is no contract yet, so there are no rights.

I deeply appreciate your interest in this book and your personal involvement in offering to prepare a new typescript of the pages sent to you and for putting up $50 of your own money if asked. However, we are not ready for such offers, believe me, but I promise to keep them in mind when the manuscript in English is finalized.

So, please Mr. Herdeck, do nothing further right now along the lines of your proposals. You have my word that I will make contact with you again when this thing gets off the ground.

Yours sincerely,

R.C. Markham

cc: Dr. Hartwig, USA

Mr. John Allen, Arusha

19 FEBRUARY 1973 MARKHAM TO ALLEN

Dear John,

BW. MYOMBEKERE and BI. BUGONOKA

I have been working on your tapes and have the following information for you:

    Part 1. Pp 122 – 255, which is the end of part 1, were sent to Aniceti for editing and for sending on to you. Have you received these from him? If not will you please write to him asking him for a little haste.

    Pages 1 to 121 are already edited and waiting to be sent onto London for reading.

    Part 2. We have pages 250 – 310 on typescript. It would be easier if we called these pages 1 to 54 or part 2. We also have 2 ½ used tapes to return to you and I want to know if you have need of them? At the moment we have 2 ½ (five sides) to go onto typescript and I would like to know what else you have for us on tape.

    There has been a temporary hold-up due to the lack of a typist but I hope things will improve. Nothing from Ford F. as yet!

Yours sincerely,

R.C. Markham

cc Dr. G. Hartwig USA

22 FEBRUARY 1973 KITEREZA TO LARSON

Dear Miss Larson,

Thanks for your letter of 23 February 1973, with the two tubes of BenGay which reached me on the 10th of March '73. Fr van der Wee also brought your check of $10 so that I can buy Andrews Liver Salt and aspirin obtainable here. He will purchase it and bring it.

    You asked how I am. Indeed, I am better because the BenGay helps so much. I use it when my joints are really hurting. Please tell your aunt, Henrietta, that the medicine she sent for dysentery is very helpful.

    I understand that Mrs. Shoonie has written about music here on our island of Ukerewe and that it is published.

    Please greet all of your family, wishing them a blessed Easter from me and my wife! Our love to you.

Aniceti Kitereza

---

2 April 1973 Kitereza to Hartwig Dear

Dr. Hartwig!

Your letter of 23 February arrived 11 March '73 along with a personal monthly plan book that Mama Shoonie found for me. Thank you very much for it will remind me of the days!

Your work at Duke University is very hard along with your writing about the Bakerebe. On 29 March '73, I received a letter from Fr Deschamps in Canada. He is very happy to be with his family and to get hearing aids. He also sends his hope that my book will soon be available. But what shall I tell him?!

On 26 Feb '73, I welcomed a guest who stayed in the U.S. for six years. He slept here at my home. His name is Fr Alexander Mugonya. His relative, Bernardini Buyanza is the elder who helped you a great deal in your research. He will hope to read your article in HISTORICAL RESEARCH when he travels to London.

Anna and I send you our best wishes for a blessed Easter. Your friend,

Aniceti Kitereza

---

23 May 1973 Markham to Allen

Dear John,

BWANA MYOMBEKERE AND BIBI BUGONOKA

In a recent letter to you I mentioned a visit to Miss Susan Fisher of the Ford Foundation, Nairobi which was at her request.

I have put our discussions into the form of an aide-memoire which I attach. Apart from one small alteration on joint publishing, Miss Fisher agrees with it in principle.

You were talked about at length and I feel your ears were hot that day. You will read that you will be asked to do the job of translation back into a Swahili which will be accepted by the Institute, and in this connection I have to quote from your letter to me of 17.11.73, after you had heard that I would try for a subsidy and would itemize estimate a translation fee of 250 Pounds in my application.

> *"My point was the IF you put in an editor's fee in the subsidy estimate, you cannot use it for another purpose. So either you would have to return it or I should pass it straight to Aniceti.*

> *I should prefer you not to include it in your estimate and to stick to my contractual 1/-. I do not like to be involved in what you call a fib. Nor do I like to appear to undervalue my own work in this way. 1/- is an obvious sacrifice: 250 is apparently underpayment. The difference is of importance if later I want to accept a fee for other work."*

It may not now be necessary for me to fib as I gather that I need not itemize or break down into detail. We would receive a subsidy in total.

The position at the moment is that I did the corrections. I am two-thirds finished and will definitely complete Part 1 and take it to London with me on 16th June. As you know this is a labour of love done in my house in the evening and week-ends.

What of you? Do you wish to partake? If you prefer not to do the translation owing to your recent long illness, would you recommend Hammiss Kitumboy or another? Please let me know how you feel about everything.

Yours sincerely,

R. C. Markham cc: Dr. G. Hartwig

(attachment of minutes from meeting with Ford Foundation)

Aide-memoire of a meeting on May 3rd at Silopark House, Nairobi, between Miss Susan

B. Fisher, Assistant to the Representative for Eastern and Southern Africa of the Ford Foundation and R.C. Markham, Managing Director of Heinemann Educational Books (E.A.) Ltd.

Subject: Aniceti Kitereza's book Bwana Myombekere and Bibi Bugonoka

History: Knowledge of the book reached Ford Foundation in New York via Gerald Hartwig who first brought to H.E.B. notice existence of book in Swahili. Hartwig sent RCM manuscript in Swahili in 2 parts. Manuscript ready by John Allen who showed deep interest and enthusiasm. MS sent to Institute of Swahili Research in Dar es Salaam for opinions on publication but rejected on grounds that Swahili old-fashioned, too verbose, not following new national pattern. Their verdict argued and queried by JA and RCM but all arguments over-ruled. Then decided by HEB that JA transliterates onto tape English translation of Swahili original and tapes are put on to typescript.

Also decided to make 2 books in English as one volume far too long. To date, Part 1 fully on typescript and one-third of Part 2. Such typescripts

badly in need of editing. Part 1 fully edited and being re-typed. Part 2 not touched.

H.E.B. views and policy: RCM shares JA's enthusiasm for publication of book. We feel English translation is a must for inclusion in African Writers Series, published by parent company in London. London appreciate local enthusiasm but refuse promises publication until typescript in their hands and reader opinion sought in London. RCM will send London finished typescript of PART 1 (which is separate entity for book) and await their decision. If yes, no problems. If no, RCM will publish here.

Swahili edition: As Institute of Swahili Research rejected original Swahili content RCM feels that if Part 1 of English work published either in London or Nairobi, we translate published English work back into Swahili and publish. Problems would be possible lack of interest and small sale of English edition in East Africa resulting in rethink of Swahili edition, areas of sale being only Tanzania and Kenya Coast. Obvious translator of work from English to Swahili is JA who from start has been emotionally involved in work and has taken great trouble to visit author twice in remote part of Lake islands. In event of his refusal we seek another scholar not so emotionally involved but with appreciation of author's special qualities of choice of word and inherent sincerity.

General: The book must be divided into two parts, second part having continuity but Part 1 can be published as entity. If London publish Part 1 in English we would publish it in Swahili. Anything published by HEB Nairobi must have received HEB London's blessing. Minute chance London may refuse publish in English. If HEB Nairobi publish English and/or Swahili editions, we need subsidy, based on short publishing runs with pro rate high printer's bills and great need to keep price down to boost market in limited areas of sale. If London publish, book reaches international markets worldwide. If we publish, markets shrink to East Africa only.

F.F. View and possible policy: FF shows enthusiasm for book and therefore for award of subsidy to HEB for publication. Subsidy would be given on strict understanding Swahili edition is published later. Subsidy for English edition given first but only if HEB Nairobi publish. No subsidy to London if they publish English work. In Swahili edition,

FF prefer Aniceti's content not to suffer by professional translator so wish JA to be commissioned. JA to translate English version back to reasonably modern Swahili accepted by Institute. He should not edit down original Swahili manuscript. In event London refusing publish Part 1 in English,

RCM obtains quotations local printers for runs of publish Part 1 in English, RCM obtains quotations local printers for runs of 3000 to 5000, works out estimates based on printers' quotations and taking in HEB working profit, royalty to author and discounts to booksellers, and puts up to FF these estimates showing published prices without subsidy and grades of published prices with varying amounts of subsidy. FF to examine and decide. For Swahili edition, FF prefers possible tie-up of joint publication with Institute of Swahili Research, which, if Swahili acceptable, would sway sales.

Finis: RCM explained we are commercial publishers and expect to make profits on all publications; if Aniceti Kitereza is to be published in Nairobi there is reasonable doubt of publishing success and profit. Subsidy therefore vitally necessary for English and Swahili editions. Award of subsidy will not relax our sales efforts nor dim enthusiasm. We attack as for any book with HEB imprint, conscientiously and for reward.

Therefore, with Swahili edition we would prefer tie-up with like commercial publishers with viable distribution systems in Tanzania and not the Institute with ivory tower ideals and complete lack commercial push.

May '73 Hartwig to Larson (hand written)

Dear Emily:

I received the enclosed news from Markham in Nairobi yesterday. My impression is that things are now clicking at long last for Aniceti's manuscript. I had given up on Ford; it must have taken them four months to make the initial contact. I am relieved that Markham has been taken off the hook regarding expenses. John Allen persuaded him to extend himself far beyond reasonable limits. Too bad Aniceti is not able to appreciate how he has influenced so many people to work on his behalf. Quite a man!

The summer activities are looming and I'm desperately trying to complete a writing project during the next ten days. Being torn in three or four directions simultaneously is not to my liking nor do I have the necessary energy for it. Nonetheless, one always seems to end up doing that sort of thing.

Enclosed is a list of books I hope the participants will get around to reading before you arrive. They will also be expected to get into the library resources. More later.

Best wishes,

Jerry

MAY 1973 HARTWIG TO MARKHAM

Dear Mr. Markham,

What a relief to receive information about the most recent developments in respect to Bwana Myombekere *and* Bibi Bugonoka. *I suppose it is correct to assume that you had given up on the Ford Foundation as I had. Ford's interest gives the project vital support at a critical time.*

I wish you well as you take Part I to London. It certainly belongs in the African Writers Series where it could be more readily disseminated.

I am sorry to learn of John Allen's illness. It would be unfortunate for Aniceti if he was unable to do the Swahili edition although his contribution to this project is already enormous.

Best wishes, Gerald Hartwig

18 AUGUST 1973 MARKHAM TO ALLEN

Dear John: A KEREBE TALE (as I now prefer to call it)

As I told you in my letter of June 4th, I intended to take Part 1 to London with me and finish off the final typing of the edited version in my London office. Famous last words! I brought it back in the same state as I took it.

However, since my return to Nairobi about 2 weeks ago, I have worked at it and can now announce with pleasure that Part 1 is now ready for sending to London and this will be done by air mail very shortly as soon as my own editorial staff have browsed through it.

There is one original of Part 1 typescript and 2 copies. The original goes to London and one copy is being posted to you in Arusha. I support it ought to go direct to the author but as you have been very much involved I have chosen you. No doubt you will want to send it on to Aniceti.

At this stage I wish to send to London only the text as it now stands. The question of illustrations, glossaries, etc. can come later. The second carbon copy of Part 1 is being sent to Miss Fisher of the Ford Foundation, Nairobi, but I must warn her it is on loan and must be returned to me. If she wishes to make herself page xeroxes then she may do so.

Now for Part II. While I was away in UK I paid a European girl Shs. 5/ per page for transferring your tapes to typescript. She finished the lot, all 203 pages, so we now have Part II on typescript. I have 6 large tapes and 2 small which are all yours and will keep them here until you ask for them. Unfortunately she typed only 1 original and 11 copy so I have decided to send you both leaving me with none. No doubt you will send one or both to Aniceti for his primary editing. Eventually it will be returned to me and will be shelved until we know finally the publishing outcome of Part 1.

It is possible that we arrange the disposal of manuscripts differently so I hope you will not mind my sending them to you and you doing the distribution as you think fit.

You will probably have comments on the final version of Part 1 and perhaps the author will also. If this is the case try to get them to me as soon as possible.

We now sit back with crossed fingers.

Yours sincerely,

RC Markham

cc: Aniceti Kitereza, Dr. Gerald Hartwig, Miss S.B. Fisher

---

25 August 1973 Kitereza to Larson

Dear Miss Emilie:

Your letter of 8 July 1973 I received on 25 July '73. Here in my house, we were happy to hear that you are well. As for us, we continue as before. Thank you for writing about this long delay with my book that causes great sadness.

That your nephew has not written me since your visit is not a problem. Perhaps he hesitates because I am an old man – 77 years! I was glad to read about your trip to Durham and your time with Jerry and Shoonie. The seminar you joined with fourteen middle school teachers is to develop reading materials about Africa. That is hard work!

Fr van der Wee brought your check of $15 along with medicines. I will itemize for you as there is custom duty to be paid out.

I particularly appreciated reading that you are enjoying the fish tilapia which we have in great abundance here in Lake Victoria. Here they are very large.

May all be well with you. Greetings also from my wife Anna.

Your friend,

Aniceti Kitereza

2 DECEMBER 1973

Dear Emilie Larson:

Four months have passed and I have not had a letter from you since 8 July. I did respond in August 25th.

It grieves me with no news from you and I hope you are not ill. Now it is soon Christmas and so I send you greetings. Please, if you can, send me another calendar for 1974! My wife, Anna Katura, also sends greetings to you.

Your friend,

Aniceti Kitereza

1974

This is a turbulent year. Aniceti's failing health is compounded with national policies threatening his and Anna's well being. Survival of the book is another issue.

Dear Miss Emilie Larson:

Your letter of 25 November '73 arrived 24 December '73 and also your check of $15 to celebrate Christmas and the new year of '74. I pray God to give you a long life and that your health is good.

I wrote two letters but with no answer! In one I asked if you could send me a calendar for 1974. The wall calendar is very good like last year.

I heard from Dr. Hartwig that he heard from a publisher regarding his book, and that they rejected it. Loo!! Do you know why? You also wrote that the Hartwigs work very hard. They have a program which includes their three oldest children. Mama Shoonie has 28 piano students – she is very talented. And when she sings, her voice brings pleasure to all.

I was very surprised to read that you have a garden and that you must water your plants when it is hot.

My rheumatism is in my whole body; these days I am unable to walk. From your beloved friends

Mr. and Mrs. A. Kitereza

28 January 1974 Hartwig to Markham

Dear Mr. Markham:

I thought you would be interested in seeing the biographical data on Kitereza from the perspective of Donald Herdeck in his extensive guide to African Authors. I will send a copy of this to Kitereza who will not be impressed by the printing errors. He is still a school- master at heart!

I have not heard anything concerning A Kerebe Tale since August. Is it possible to get an indication of progress at this time? I would certainly appreciate it.

Best wishes, Gerald Hartwig

---

5 February 1974 Markham to Hartwig Dear

Dr. Hartwig:

A KEREBE TALE

Many thanks for your letter of January 28th with which you sent me Herdeck's quote about Aniceti from his guide to African authors. What a spiel! I agree with you that Aniceti will not take too kindly towards it. Herdeck has somewhat jumped the gun, of course.

Here we have yet another tale of woe and delay, delay, delay. I am very upset that this time the delay has been caused by two African academics, local chaps, and they have treated this manuscript and me in a very casual way.

The MS was read by two Europeans in the UK, one an Africanist who rejected it and another, a one-time Professor of Literature in Nairobi, who suggested publication with minor alterations. My London office weighed both reports and came back to me to offer it to two African literary men whom we knew well. This was last October, and despite letters, reminders, telegrams, phone calls, all sorts of pleas, they both have not come up with reports yet.

I went to UK for 10 days over Christmas and both readers had promised me I could take their reports with me. No such luck! I was to discuss the issue with the London editorial board but could do nothing in the circumstances.

Until these two gentlemen come up with reports the issue of publication is in limbo. I will continue to struggle with them and hope that one day soon I can let you know the outcome. Until then –

Best wishes,

Yours sincerely,

RC Markham

---

27 February 1974 Hartwig to Markham

Dear Mr. Markham:

Thank you very much for sending your reader's assessment to me. Since I have never read Aniceti's original, I am in no position to comment on the validity of the reader's assumption that Aniceti was in fact a pretender. This, however, could be determined without too much difficulty.

I am unable to determine the knowledge and background of the reader from his comments. But it is clearly evident that his understanding of literature is restricted to that of his own cultural milieu, and then to that of the literate realm. Whether he discusses biography, history, ethnography, the novel or chronicles, his base of measurement is European. It is one of the finest contemporary examples of what Professor Daniel Kunene has labeled "deculturation" i.e.. if the African product does not fit the European conception of what it should be, then it is inferior and fit only for local consumption; hence, publish it in Swahili. My contention would be that if it is suitable for publication in Swahili then it is suitable for publication in English.

Because Aniceti was never trained to write a novel or a history or an ethnography, it is not all together surprising that his "story of the Old Kerebe" does not fit into one of these categories. Nor should it. The value of his work is certainly that he was concerned about specific issues at a particular time in history It is true that these issues tended to be parochial in nature—that was his world—but it is equally true that the vast majority of his generation in Africa experienced similar problems. It is more likely that he treats universal themes within a local context.

As for the comments regarding the significance of the Kerebe or one of their rulers in the history of Tanzania, this is totally inaccurate as well as irrelevant. The Kerebe, I cynically contend, will become important when my ms. about them is published. What is historically significant is what is made significant simply by capturing a portion of the past. What is not preserved can never be historically significant. I personally respect Aniceti greatly for his attempt to preserve a portion of the past.

Simultaneously it is mandatory to have an introduction that places the story in a comprehensible context. Nor can it necessarily conform to present <u>ujamaa</u> principles. It was conceived at a different time for different purposes. Just as Nyerere has selected certain traditional practices for inclusion within the ujamaa framework, so too has Aniceti selected certain traditions for emphasis for his purposes.

Incidentally, your reader overlooked the genre of oral literature (folklore) and this is where Aniceti must be partially assessed. He is a marginal man in many ways, including how he writes. He does not fit neatly into this or that category. For that reason alone, his work has considerable merit.

I am sorry, but the cultural bias conveyed in the reader's statement rather overwhelmed me. It stems from a tradition that insured Aniceti could become no more than a clerk in his lifetime.

If there is anything I can do to be of assistance, please let me know. The value of the ms. is obviously enhanced by this Reader's Report. Carry on!

Best wishes,

Gerald Hartwig

---

15 MARCH 1974 ALLEN TO HARTWIG

Dear Dr. Hartwig:

I have not seen Markham since he received the report, because first I and then he have been away. Meanwhile he has written to Aniceti turning the book down and my first act on return was to write to Aniceti to say that I should persevere. Then I received gratefully from Markham your letter to him – a letter which, if I may say so without impertinence, I find thoughtful and wise. I will go through it and make a few comments in the order of your points.

That Aniceti is or ever was a pretender is nonsense. When (1953-58) I was Deputy Provincial Commissioner, Mwanza, I never heard of Aniceti; but I knew the Omukama Lukumbuzya quite well and should unquestionably have heard of any present or past pretender.

I can identify the author of the report with fair certainty as one of three persons, all violently anti-European and specifically anti-Allen, while slavishly imitating all things European. One of them I heard begin a speech - "At UDSM we teach the students to read, write and appreciate Socialist Literature." There is no need to say more.

I have always urged Markham to publish in English first. I believe that the book would today appeal more to the English reading public. The African public does not – yet – see any point in reading about any but his own tribe. Hence Wakilindi, which was publishined simultaneously in English and Swahili, has sold better in English. Aniceti's book could not be published simultaneously in both languages, because Swahili is not Aniceti's language and his translation into it was written in great haste and is full of omissions of half or whole words and grammatical errors. To make a fair copy would take me a very long time and I would not entrust the work to anyone else, because I find that everyone whom I have tried alters too much and ruins the style. With Wakilindi it was quite different. Before beginning the translation I had to make an entirely fresh transliteration of the original from Arabic script, so that was ready first. My contention, to adapt your wording is that it is suitable for publication in English now, and later in Swahili, when the English edition has made a reputation and/or the Swahili reading public has advanced further in liberal education.

Your para 3. The reader asks for totally contradictory changes and these comments make no logical sense. It is not, however, true to say that A is concerned about . . . a particular time in history. In my translator's introduction I have, with Aniceti's consent said that it would be a mistake to put a definite date on Myombekere. He had dated it to the XVI century; but he has included mention of Europeans (XIX C) Luo, bananas and cassava, very difficult to date, and some fish introduced to the lake in C XX. He has treated universal themes within a local context in place but not in time.

Your para 4. I entirely agree. See my comments above.

Your para 5. I think it possible that one of the reader's unexpressed objections may be that Aniceti, by drawing attention to the the success of the old ideas of ujamaa, does hint at the comparative failure of the sham ujamaa is now being so strongly pressed.

Your para 7. I agree

Your para 8. I regret that the tradition persists to this day. I have a much younger friend who is one of the finest younger Swahili scholars and and poets now alive. His western education is slight and he is and will always remain a clerk.

Your last Para. I am sure that there is something you can do to help. The first is to write to Aniceti, who must be very sad and tell him not to despair. Then you and I must consider how to get started again without Heinemann. Here I will add that you should know the position between Heinemann and me. Bob Markham is a great personal friend; but in business matters we do not agree at all. When Heinemann, on Bob's advice accepted my book, "Tendi", I wanted a cheap series in Swahili only and to this they agreed and it has come out. I also wanted a cheap paperback English edition and to this they agreed; but later very much against my advice they insisted on an English and Swahili Edition so expensive that it cannot possibly sell except to a few libraries. It does not sell and of course they have forgotten that this was against my advice, so they have now no faith in my opinion.

I feel now that if we try any of the publishers represented in E Africa, they will either see the present comments or send it for comment to similar people. I know that Bob did raise an interest in a subsidy from one of the foundations; but until I see him, I cannot say which. I am sure that Bob will write off his present loss and let me have the typescripts for any use that you and I can make of them. I will get in touch with the local representative of the foundation and find out their position. Then I will write again. Meanwhile, please consider the best course of action. I do not know at all what pull you have with American publishers or what their reactions would be.

The present position of the translation is as follows: Part I typed and faired, corrected by both Aniceti and me. Part II typed and in Aniceti's hands for correction. Glossary and notes in draft with Aniceti for correction. There are not many queries that are likely to be answered so this means that all that is needed is for a fair copy to be made (by me) when he returns it.

Of Part I there are three copies; of Pt II unfortunately only two.

I think that I have said all that I can to bring you up to date. Do please assume that I will do anything in my power to help. On my own behalf and even more on Aniceti's I am most grateful to you.

Yours very sincerely,

John Allen

25 MARCH 1974 MARKHAM TO ALL CORRESPONDERS

BWANA MYOMBEKERE AND BIBI BUGONOKA

(latterly known as A KEREBE TALE

by Aniceti Kitereza

ANNOUNCEMENT TO INTERESTED PARTIES BY RC MARKHAM

It is with desperation and the greatest reluctance that I have to announce the decision of my Company not to progress with publication of the above work. This decision includes the work in English, in its original Swahili and in any new form of Swahili.

Many factors come into this and I will try to list them as they all influenced the decision made by my fellow Directors and myself at a full Board meeting held in Nairobi recently, at which senior Directors from H.E.B. International were present. At any Board meeting the majority decision counts.

I think it is apt that I recapitulate a little on the history of this work before I go into the reasons for non-publication.

In October, 1970, Gerald Hartwig sent me the photo-copies of Aniceti's handwritten manuscript in Swahili which was in two parts. This MS was read by John Allen who showed deep interest and enthusiasm. The MS was sent to the Institute of Swahili Research in the University of Dar es Salaam for their opinions on publication but they rejected it on the grounds that Aniceti's Swahili was old-fashioned and did not follow the new national pattern of the language emerging from the political structure of the country.

John Allen and I decided to produce a manuscript in English from Aniceti's Swahili, so John transliterated on to tape an English translation from the original Swahili and the tapes were put into typescript. These typescripts had to be drastically edited and as, even with editing, the two parts were far too long to publish in one book, it was decided to make two books, Part 1 of which would be published first with a gap before Part II came out.

I must point out that John Allen in his enthusiasm, purchased with his own money an RCA Victor tape recorder with accessories, when this machine did not satisfy him, purchased a smaller but better machine, again from his own pocket. Heinemann, on the other hand, purchased several tapes for these machines and financed two safaris for John to visit the author in far-off Ukerewe Island in his own car. Heinemann also financed professional typists to put the work on to typescript and sent the author money from time to time. I am certain that John Allen is out of pocket as many of his outlays came from the heart and not the hand.

When one observes the date it was first offered, 1970, and the date of this report, one justifiably wonders why all the delays. It is extremely significant that all delays in the assessing of this work came from outside people, mainly African I am sorry to say, who caused me much distress in my endeavour to obtain reports and/or the return of the manuscript. It is sad to note that the Tanzanian African appears disinterested in historical matter emanating from within Tanzania from an area and culture on which little, if anything, is known and in print.

It can be appreciated that such delays and rebuffs dampened my own enthusiasm and gave me cause for concern over the book's reception by Tanzanians if published.

However, I did not give up.

Publishers invariably rely not only on their own enthusiasm of a book in the house but on Readers' opinions and reports. One tries to pick Readers from the field of the subject matter of the book though in Aniceti's case this was difficult.

The MS of Part I, in English and personally edited by me, was sent to Heinemann, London, and a Reader was found, highly esteemed for his previous reports on books by Africans and about Africa in literary and historic fields. He advised rejection of the MS in a very fair and unbiased report.

At my request, it was then sent to an ex-Professor of Literature at Nairobi, currently lecturing in African literature in Leeds. He suggested that London take a chance on publication but he was very half-hearted.

Based on these two well-thought out and constructive reports, London decided not to publish in the U.K. which meant that its inclusion in our African Writers Series was definitely out. I was told I could go ahead and obtain local reports and that, based on positive reactions from a few Readers, I would have London's blessing to publish in English in Nairobi.

Alas! Two African academics, one a practicing school teacher of history and an Administrator all read the manuscript of Part I and tore it to shreds. I am not in office to argue with any Reader who has presented a report, but in office I can quietly appraise, despise, accept, reject, such reports and analyze them specifically with a view to publication. At heart, I am a commercial publisher, willing to take a calculated risk but also cognizant of a possible failure, and failures we do not like.

Hence, the discussion on the publication of Part I of Aniceti's book was thrust at an editorial Board meeting of H.E.B. East Africa recently and the majority of Directors voted against its publication, not only in English but in Swahili. I hang my head in shame, but as a Director, accept the decision of the Board.

Why do we not publish? The Ford Foundation from its Nairobi office would possibly subsidize the English edition based on our firm promise that a Swahili edition would be published later. A subsidy would possibly pay the printer's bill but would not sell the the book. My two travellers did a form of market research in parts of Kenya and Tanzania and little enthusiasm was shown by what is known as "the trade" towards such a book. It has a limited appeal and the possible purchaser of a book in Dar es Salaam or Tanga would not necessarily wish to read about the Kerebe tribe if a similar work on a tribe nearer to them were available. My travellers returned with a somewhat negative report of possible sale, and, after all, sales make the wheels of any commercial publishing house turn.

If the book was published for a small market on a short print-run it would possibly be priced at Shs. 15/- per copy, even with a possible subsidy. On a long print-run, Shs. 14/- per copy. Where, then, its purchasing pull at such prices? We all know the reaction of the Regional Education Officer in Mwanza who was far "too busy" to read the MS, and would therefore be the last person to recommend the work to schools in the Region. If this book is to be relegated to what we know as a "single copy, passer-by, bookshop" sale my Company are not willing to publish it, and my Company cannot visualize large sales from other sources, especially Dar es Salaam and other East African Universities.

An American edition is a doubtful starter.

We must then be realistic and not attempt to publish just because a handful of enthusiasts are eager. On this even I have to be firm.

This therefore brings me to appreciations of personalities involved in this effort towards publication of a dedicated work.

The author: Aniceti Kitereza

His world might possibly collapse because of our decision. An old, arthritic, busy, involved man, desperate to put on record the history of his tribe, confident that his fellow Africans would want such a history in any presentable form and failing to understand why they reject it, relying on the integrity of an international publisher to produce and publish his work, only to reject it because of publishing economics. To him I say sorry and mean it. He has the authority and alternative to offer his books to another publisher but this is short shrift and, possibly, a reprehensible suggestion after nearly four years of working with and for Heinemann.

<u>*The translator: John Allen*</u>

The man who has done all the work, who made himself ill by fitting the work of this translation in his other Swahili interests, who went out of his way to make the thing a reality, by spending his own money out of a love for the Swahili language, and because of his great belief in Aniceti's talents. I have a conscience bout John because he had a conscience about this book. His purchases, his trips to Nansio, his living in cramped quarters on the Island, his interesting conversations with the author, his unrevealed cash out-lays, his honesty and his ideas on which shape the book should take, all come to naught. I am deeply in his debt and I hope I can make amends somehow, though I doubt it.

Gerald Hartwig

He went out of his way in the USA to interest several organizations in the financial subsidization of this work and due to his great interest and belief, introduced the Ford Foundation to the idea and to me. I thank him for his continued belief in the publication of this book and for his introduction of the idea in the first place. He, too, must be out of pocket.

Ford Foundation, Nairobi (Miss Susan Fisher)

I seem to have reneged on my original promise that even if London refused to publish in English, I would. Forgive me for changing my outlook but a certain amount of coercion was involved. I am sorry that the idea of publication is just not on, even though a subsidy from her Foundation would have spread butter on the bread. My grateful thanks to her and her organization for the offer of a subsidy and for their belief in the work to be published.

I must add that we too, in Heinemann, Nairobi, had belief in the work and there is a large sum on our books which is on the debit side of the production account of this work. This will now be written off, as will the work of our secretaries, temporary typists, editors and Managing Director, all of whom worked unstintingly out of office hours so that Aniceti's book should be brought out. What a great shame the whole effort cam to nothing.

I have typescripts belonging to the author, tapes and photographs belonging to the translator, illustrations belonging to Gerald Hartwig, etc. etc. Perhaps I could be informed and instructed where to send them. To John Allen, I insist that Heinemann, Nairobi, purchase his RCA Victor tape recorder and accessories and tapes, and that our cheque will be sent to him shortly. His machine will enhance our Nairobi offices and will be used for our other work. It will constantly remind me of him and his efforts to get Aniceti published.

This seems to be the end of this announcement and of this saga. My thanks are also due to my London office for their initial help and encouragement and understanding. I offer no thanks to the local Readers nor to the other individuals who delayed, spurned and rejected the publishing of Aniceti's work.

RC Markham

Distribution: Kitereza, Allen, Hartwig, Fisher, Van der Wee, Currey

---

25 MARCH 1974 HARTWIG TO ALLEN

Dear Mr. Allen:

I was naturally upset to receive your letter today concerning the present status of Aniceti's manuscript. Thus far I have heard nothing official from Markham but I trust I will in the near future. There is far too much invested in this endeavor to despair now so I shall proceed to knock on doors here. Incidentally, it is the Ford Foundation that expressed interest in the ms: Miss Susan Fisher, The Ford Foundation P.O. Box 1081 Nairobi.

The potential interest of Ford was through a contact made by me in New York. Hence the pullout of Heinemann should not be critical unless there are compelling local political reasons for Ford's timidity along with that of publishers. But I think you could clarify the basic literary nature of the ms with Miss Fisher without great difficulty.

Beyond establishing contact with Miss Fisher, it would aid me enormously if I had a copy of the ms here, at least Part I and Part II whenever available. I can get it duplicated here and then proceed to make contacts with several potential publishers. I feel that a subsidy becomes all the more imperative for the English edition, particularly if a publisher here were to undertake the project, otherwise the cost will be prohibitive. Paperback editions for a commercial publisher in the US need potential sales of around 15,000 to be considered for publication!

I'll start thinking about options here and look forward to hearing from you in the near future.

Sincerely,

Gerald Hartwig

27 MARCH 1974 HARTWIG TO MARKHAM

Dear Mr. Markham:

On March 15th John Allen wrote to inform me that Kitereza's manuscript was now rejected by Heinemann. If that information is correct I would certainly appreciate learning from you the background for the decision. In addition, any advice you can pass along to me concerning the manuscript would certainly be welcomed.

I have asked John to forward a copy of Part I to me so I can enquire here in the States about the possibility of publishing it. I imagine he has already discussed the situation with you. It may well be that publishing it outside East Africa is a probable course to follow. Naturally I'm concerned by the Ford Foundation's role because the need for subsidy will not decrease simply by publishing it here.

I respect your position in this matter and sincerely trust that a way out can be found.

Sincerely,

Gerald Hartwig

27 MARCH 1974 HARTWIG TO KITEREZA

Dear Aniceti:

I have just received word from John Allen that Heinemann's is not going to publish your manuscript. Thus far I have heard no official word from Markham. Therefore, I am not sure what the actual status is because Markham has always written about more than one option.

I am upset by Allen's letter and am now waiting for word from Markham. If Allen's information is correct, we shall look for another publisher, maybe here in the United States. I thought it would be published this year, but it may not be until next year.

Please be assured, it will be published! Best wishes,

Gerald Hartwig

4 APRIL 1974 MARKHAM TO HARTWIG

Dear Dr. Hartwig:

I have received your letter of March 27th with some surprise as you inform me that on March 15th, John Allen told you that we had rejected Kitereza's book.

Since writing your letter of March 27th, you have probably received my 5- page effort dated March 25th and I can assure you that this was the first intimation I gave to all people connected which is quite unfair of him.

I now await reactions from everybody to whom my apologia was sent, especially regarding the return, to the rightful owners, of the manuscripts and photographs.

May I say, once again, that I am desperately sorry on what has happened to Aniceti's work. Just for the record, I have been waiting for a meeting with John Allen since he received my letter of March 25th but to date he has remained quiet even though he is living in Nairobi. I suppose it is now up to me to approach him.

Yours sincerely,

R.C. Markham

---

20 April 1974 Kitereza to Hartwig

Dear Dr. Gerald Hartwig,

Your letter of 27 March 1974 I received on 7 April 1974.

I must tell you that my very revered relative, Bernardino Buyanza who was very important in your Ukerewe research, died on 2 February 1974.

You have read the letter from John Allen that Heinemanns will not continue to consider publishing my book. I received the announcement as well on 1 April '74. This is bad news, Mr. Hartwig! Maybe in the USA?! Have you received this announcement? Please write me as soon as you can.

My wife, Anna Katura, sends greetings to all. Miss Emilie wrote on March 24, 1974 that she will send help for us to buy food. It is very expensive now and my rheumatism continues.

Shoonie and the children, greet them!

Your friend, Aniceti Kitereza

---

22 April 1974 Hartwig to Markham

Dear Mr. Markham:

I have read with considerable concern your letters of March 25th and April 4th. Although John Allen jumped the gun I was not caught completely off-guard, given the one reader's comment.

I am comewhat puzzled about Allen's next move. When I responded to him earlier, I suggested he send a copy of the English ms to me. Then I could check with colleagues of mine in the field of African literature for comments. Concomitantly I wanted him to check with the Ford Foundation representative to determine if support for a possible subsidy continued to exist. At the time I offered those suggestions your 50 page effort had not yet arrived. However, aside from ego bruises for all concerned, I see no barrier to pursuing the enterprise if there is merit in it. Both you and Allen have invested a wealth of time and energy in the ms and it has no doubt been enhanced thereby. The decision not to publish was obviously based on a number of factors which I can appreciate. But I also regard it within its corporate context. More important to me is what your personal judgment of the ms is. Would you support, for literary and content reasons, the publication of the ms by some other publishing company?

Incidentally, I have not heard from John since March 15th so I am as much in the dark about his attitudes and his possible course of action as you are. I trust he will be able to appreciate your dilemma. Nor has any recent word come from Aniceti although I wrote to him immediately promising continued support. But I am hampered given no access to the revised English ms.

Please be assured that I appreciate all that you have personally done to enhance Aniceti's work and to see it eventually published. I sincerely hope that you will remain in the background as a sympathetic supporter for whatever transpires.

Sincerely yours,

Gerald Hartwig

---

13 MAY 1974 MARKHAM TO KITEREZA

A KEREBE TALE

I have received your letter of 19th April which acknowledged receipt of my letter of apology of March 25th, 1974, and I am pleased that you have taken the announcement that H.E.B cannot publish your book.

I recently had a long talk with John Allen and we came to the conclusion that he should take over from me as your agent in Nairobi which means that in future any letters you write about your work should be addressed to John and not to this office.

At the same time, John took over from me all the manuscripts of Part I and Part 2 which had been held in this office and which had been edited in this office. I gather that he is making arrangements to endeavour to place your manuscript with another publisher

I also understand that firstly he is contacting Miss Fisher of Ford Foundation as she may be able to help with the placing of your book in other directions.

As an individual, I am still convinced that your book is worth publishing and in my private capacity, I will be only too pleased to help out with anything I can do in the way of editing or retyping of manuscripts

By copy of this letter to Dr. Hartwig, I would inform him that I received his letter of April 22nd and waited for reply after I had spoken to John Allen and I gather that John will be writing to Dr. Hartwig shortly.

By copy of this letter to Miss Fisher of the Ford Foundation, I would inform her that I gave John Allen her message and that he is contacting her this week.

Many thanks for your patience and your past trust in Heinemann Educational Books and once again I have to apologize that my company was not able to help you

Yours very sincerely,

R.C. Markham

cc: Allen, Hartwig, Fisher

---

20 MAY 1974 HARTWIG TO MARKHAM

Dear Mr. Markham:

Thank you for sending me a copy of your letter to Aniceti Kitereza, dated 13th May.

I am relieved to learn that you and John Allen have sorted out matters and that he will endeavor to see the ms in print.

To date I have heard nothing from Mr. Allen concerning what he plans to do or how he plans to do it. I can only assume that Aniceti continues to be well represented.

Again, let me express my appreciation to you for all the effort you have expended on this rather lengthy ordeal.

Sincerely yours,

Gerald Hartwig

12 JULY 1974 KITEREZA TO HARTWIG DEAR

Dr. Hartwig,

Because I haven't heard from you for a long time, I think that maybe the address is wrong? The last letter I wrote you was on 20 April '74 when I informed you of

Buyanza's death. And also the letter from Markham. John Allen wrote on 23 June '73 that he is going to England for a time but he didn't say when he returns.

Here in Tanzania the news is not good. The government has issued a new law that every person must move into a new village, even sick and old people. This is very difficult because we cannot take anything from our former house – like bati roof. I do not know what my wife and I will do for we are very poor and how will we have money to build another house? And, these days, it is very cold. I beg you to answer me!

My wife Anna Katura greets all of you with God's blessing. Greetings to Shoonie and your children. Your friend, Aniceti Kitereza

3 AUGUST 1974 FR VAN DER WEE TO LARSON

Dear Miss Emilie:

When I was in bed last night, and closing myself in the blankets, I was thinking, and asking myself how Aniceti Kitereza would feel. I visited him yesterday and found him in a most miserable situation. As you know the people have to move to new houses in villages. But they have anticipated the date by 2 weeks. So many people are not yet ready to build but had to move anyhow. So did Kitereza. As he can't walk, they moved him and his belongings in a landrover, to the place where they were building his new house. The only thing of this house I can say is that there is a roof on it, but no floor, just sand, no walls, just some poles, connected with bamboo.

On all the 4 sides it was practically open. In order to hide himself a little from the cold, he or other people had pinned up some hessian cloth, or a matte. No door yet in the house. No toilet, no place where to wash. It was a real mess, everything on the floor, no table moreover there would not be place for the table. Just a bed and a chair. If I say a mess then it is a mess. Unbelievable.

But I found him in a good mood. Well I know, thousands of people are in the same circumstances as he is, but by far most of them can help themselves. But he has no children, neither family. So everything has to be done by other people who have to be paid. He had some people working for him, but they ran away where they could gain more money. Now he is far from his fields and is afraid that the cassava will be stolen as well as his potatoes (which I believe is very true.) Happily, he has a devoted wife, but what can she do in this case?

You have written, that in case he needs something, I should let you know. I promised him to write you about his situation. And I should write as well to Jerry Hartwig, (he asked me), but unfortunately I have not got his address. Perhaps you would be so kind as to inform him. In case that something should be done, then now is the time.

Is there no possibility that he gets an advance for the book which is going to be printed? The only advantage of his moving is for me, that I have not to go so far as before, and especially not to go bare foot through a river every time. But that does not give a solution for his problem. So for today I leave it here.

Best wishes, and please think it over. Yours. Fr. Van der Wee

---

6 AUGUST 1974 HARTWIG TO KITEREZA

Dear Aniceti:

First let me apologize for not having written sooner. The excuse I gave to myself was that I always wanted to wait until there was good news to report.

In a separate envelope I am sending a copy of this letter and an advertisement for a book on African authors that has just been published. I was very surprised when I opened this up to see your picture! The author, Donald Herdeck, wrote to me last year and enquired about you after he saw the article about you in Research in African Literatures. I provided him with the picture. But I was disappointed to see numerous spelling errors – it is an imperfect world that we live in!

I have heard nothing from John Allen for at least a year. What he is now doing with your manuscript and with the Ford Foundation, I simply do not know. I wanted a copy of the English translation. I think I requested that from Markham but he gave everything to Allen. I am sure Allen is trying to find an English publisher now. Thank you for sending me his address. I shall write to him there and ask him for news.

News about my writing is finally improving. A publisher in New York will publish my study of the Kerebe within eight months. The title is not definite yet but it will be something like this: "Consequences of Trade in East Africa: The Kerebe Art of Survival, 1800 – 1895.

I am sorry to learn that you must soon move into a new house. It will be very hard for you and Anna. I trust that the people in the new village will help you in constructing a new home since you and Anna are unable to do it yourselves.

I shall write to John Allen this week and ask him what is happening. Do not worry. The book will be published.

Best wishes to you and Anna. The Hartwig family is doing well. The children begin school again in another two weeks after their three- month summer vacation.

Sincerely, Gerald Hartwig

---

9 AUGUST 1974 HARTWIG TO ALLEN

Dear Mr. Allen:

According to Aniceti, you have returned to England and to the above address. I thought it best to re-establish communication with you to determine the status of Aniceti's manuscript.

In late June, a representative from the Ford Foundation in New York tried to contact me. He inquired about the manuscript, whether I had a copy of the English version, etc. I was out of town at the time and unable to talk directly to him. Consequently, I did not learn what the purpose behind his inquiry was. Obviously Ms. Fisher has informed the Ford people in New York about the manuscript. But I still don't understand what Ford's role is or will be.

I would appreciate learning what success you have had in finding a potential publisher. I have not made any inquiries here and shall not until I hear from you. Too many cooks...If a subsidy were available I would assume it could be published in the

U.S. The various controversies surrounding the manuscript in East Africa would, presumably, not arise here.

If you are meeting with success elsewhere, so much the better I look forward to hearing from you in the near future.

Sincerely, Gerald Hartwig

---

15 AUGUST 1974 ALLEN TO HARTWIG

Dear Dr. Hartwig:

On the same day, 9 August that you wrote to me, I was writing a very similar letter to Miss Fisher. I have been hoping to hear from her and until

I do so, I feel that there is nothing that I can do, except to try to make the position clearer to you.

If Miss Fisher is successful in getting a subsidy, it will be for a Swahili Edition and this I regret, but it is better than nothing. I should then have to make a complete revision of the Swahili text and a completely new Kerebe-Swahili glossary. This I could not do without help. I can get the help but it would mean the expenditure of a very large number of hours, which means months, and of more money than I can personally afford. It would also mean that a second photocopy of the text woud be needed for the use of my collaborator. I have therefore left my copy of the Swahili in Nairobi with Miss Fisher. If this is the decision, she will arrange with your hep (?) to have another copy made for my use.

An English edition would be from my point of view advisable, and it would also be very much quicker. I should have to make a fair copy of the glossary and the job is done. I have a copy of it here and will, if you really need it, have it photocopied in Oxford. I do rather fear the cost; but I will bear it.

If Miss Fisher is unsuccessful, I must see if there is anything that I can do here. I have two publishers in mind who might be interested; but I am not optimistic and shall be glad to hear of any ideas from you. The nonsense controversies would not affect publication in England or USA; but if you have more hope than I, I would suggest that you go ahead with your ideas immediately if we get a negative reply from Miss Fisher.

Yours sincerely, John Allen

---

17 AUGUST 1974 FR VAN DER WEE TO HARTWIG

Dear Mr. Hartwig:

Thanks so much for your letter with cheque enclosed. This afternoon I am going to Kagunguli to hand money over to Kitereza. I am sure he will be very pleased.

Also thanks from my side. You wrote in your letter about compensation. I doubt very much whether there will be any for all those who had a permanent home before. And the policy of ujamaa of helping old people like Kitereza: the only thing that they did was to fetch him at his home, put him in a landrover and brought him to his new home, which he had started to build himself.

About Maryknoll, Orbis press. I hardly know any Maryknoll Fathers here, and moreover who of them is interested in a book about Wakerewe. They have their own own tribe, language, etc. I really would not know whom to approach. Perhaps their headquarters in the States??????? Or John Allen?????

These are just a few lines to let you know my appreciation of your letter and cheque. Best wishes to your family and with your work.

Yours in Christ, Fr. van der Wee

---

31 AUGUST 1974 HARTWIG TO ALLEN

Dear Mr. Allen:

I appreciated the up-dating on Aniceti's ms. Contained in your letter of 15th August.

I am rather surprised that Miss Fisher continues to pursue the path worked out with Mr. Markham when the option is no longer possible. But I certainly relish the idea of a Swahili edition although partially aware of the personal cost to you in time, energy and money.

To expedite matters – it has now been six years since this endeavor was conceived – please duplicate the English version, indicating its stage of development. When I receive it I shall make additional copies here and commence to circulate it. I know of one publisher, In Washington, D.C., who expressed considerable interest in the ms. about 18 months ago. Other possibilities will also have to be pursued. I shall gladly assume responsibility for the duplication costs so let me know what the expenses are in Oxford.

Best wishes, Gerald Hartwig

---

7 SEPTEMBER 1974 ALLEN TO HARTWIG

Dear Dr. Hartwig:

Your kind letter of 31 August reached me today. By the same mail but under separate cover I am sending you a file containing: Translator's Introduction, Author's Introduction as edited by Markham, Part I (Myombekere) of which I have obtained a second copy. I will send you Part II (Ntulanalwo) as soon as I can have it copied.

I am not sending the Glossary. I have only a very rough copy and am awaiting instructions before I fair it as wanted. It contains some 300 words and in its present condition is intelligible only to me. I shall start making a fair copy now; but it will not be final until I know exactly what is wanted.

The attention of any reader should be drawn to the fact that Aniceti is at times both verbose and repetitive. Both he and I recognize that some excisions should be made. Indeed, as I translated, I sometimes recognized that a passage was largely repetition and, particularly in Pt II, I made some excisions straight away.

Any potential publisher should be made aware of the objections raised in DSM and which frightened Markham off. I think he sent you a copy; but if not I will do so.

I have some possible pictures: one of the author is quite good. The others are almost entirely artifacts and these would appear better as line drawings. A very large variety of baskets, pots, etc. is mentioned. In a Swahili Edition their names are best left in Kerebe.

---

14 SEPTEMBER 1974 KITEREZA TO HARTWIG DEAR

Dr. Jerry Hartwig,

Your letter of 6 August '74 arrived on 18 August '74. I understand why you waited to write me until you had good news. In the envelope you sent, I was very surprised, Mr. Hartwig, to see my picture! I understand that the publisher, Donald Herdreck, requested it but that you didn't see the errors before it was printed.

I understand that you haven't heard from John Allen, nor I. He should have the glossary for the translation of the two parts so I hope he has finished it all. I was happy to read that your book will be published. Really, Mr. Jerry, this is the first time our history has been written!

As for my new house, it is very expensive from the roof, to nails and other materials. Imagine everyone in Tanzania having to move to a new place! This is a great problem along with illness and old age. On the 27th of August, Fr van der Wee came to testify that we will all be in a Kagunguli Centre. Let us pray!

I thank you for your words of encouragement that the book will be published. Greetings from us to you, your children and Shoonie.

Your friend, Aniceti and wife

---

16 SEPTEMBER 1974 ALLEN TO HARTWIG

Dear Hartwig:

I have at last managed to get Part II copied. I went to four different firms, every one of which I found closed or closing down, before I found one to take it. I sent off the original typescript, which weighed less than half the Xerox copy! But I was rather worried by the postage. This was more than double that on Pt. I, which, weighed and assessed by a very small post office, may have been under stamped. If therefore, you receive Pt II before

Pt I, I think that we shall have to hope that Pt I will turn up in time, diverted to surface mail. I do not know how long that is likely to take.

Yours sincerely,

John Allen

---

20 September 1974 Hartwig to Fr van der Wee

Dear Father v.d. Wee,

Your letter of 31 August to Emilie Larson was forwarded to me. She has made an effort to keep me informed of Kitereza's situation since she corresponds more frequently than I do.

My wife and I would like to give you the enclosed $35 to Kitereza to help meet his expenses. Although I understand ujamaa fairly well, I wanted to think that the policy would have provided for the manpower to help people like Kitereza without compensation. Anyway, I am sure he will be able to use this small sum.

The publication of his manuscript is another matter. I am working now with John Allen to find a publisher, but it is a strange business. The manuscript itself does not fall readily into a particular category, therefore determining who might be interested in publishing it remains problematical. Therefore the idea of royalties becomes an irrelevant question because there may never be any, even if published.

A possibility that comes to mind is to submit it to Maryknoll, Orbis Press. Dr. Alyward Shorter (W.F.) has at least two titles published by them and it is apparent from the inexpensive nature of their books, that all titles are subsidized. If you know any of the Maryknoll fathers who might be able to intercede on Kitereza's behalf, it would be extremely helpful if they wrote to me about it.

With best wishes, Sincerely,

Gerald W. Hartwig

---

1 October 1974 Hartwig to Allen

Dear Mr. Allen:

I apologize in my tardy response to your letter of September 15. Both sections of the manuscript have arrived and in the order you posted them.

I still have not completed the entire manuscript. When I've achieved this, I'll compose a letter for a couple of publishers. One publisher appears particularly attractive – Orbis Books. It is a press operated by the Maryknoll Fathers in New York. They have recently published a few African titles, two by Dr. Aylward Shorter. Since the Maryknoll Fathers around Musoma have close ties with the White Fathers on Ukerewe, there may be some genuine interest there. Furthermore, their prices are most reasonable.

I'll keep you informed. Sincerely,

Gerald Hartwig.

1975

Three decades have passed since Kitereza finished MYOMBEKERE. It is six years since this publishing search began. Survival and perseverance continue though not without emotional and physical challenges.

---

10 JANUARY 1975 KITEREZA TO LARSON

Greetings to you this Noel season and our New Year of 1975. It is now 21 days since hearing from you. Your check of $50 for November and December I received when Fr van der Wee brought the money to me. Thank you! Your generosity these many years have brought great comfort midst our illness and old age. Because I have written to you and not heard back, I hope all is well with you!

Fr van der Wee goes to Europe/Holland the 15th of January. He told me that he will write you about another agent to help me with everything you do for me.

My wife sends her thanks to you. Please greet David, his family, Dr. Jerry Hartwig and his wife Shoonie! Is your snow gone yet?

Your friend, Aniceti Kitereza

---

10 APRIL 1975 KITEREZA TO LARSON

Dear Miss Larson,

I am remembering that on February 19, 1975, I wrote you a letter with thanks for your gift of $50 which you sent me on 3 February '75, delivered by Fr Charles Matte. He brought it to my house on 18 February. He is asking permission to bring me money regularly each month, so that if you *are late, I receive it anyway. Also, if you sent a check for three months this would help. Please, Miss Larson, send a quick reply so this.*

When Fr Matte visited me on 18 April, he asked if you had stopped assisting me. But I replied that I had not heard such news from you. He was surprised and said that perhaps the post lost the letter. So he will write you about this.

On 21 February '75, Mr. John and wife Winifred visited me with news of the Swahili edition of my book. They stayed three days and slept at the Murutunguru Parish, returning to Nairobi, Kenya.

Here in Kagunguli Centre, I have been so very ill, near death. It began 1 March – a high fever; I couldn't walk or sleep. My body refused to leave my bed to go outside. My wife tried to help me and prayed to God until we got outside. Then I began to vomit and I fell down, right on my face. When we got back into our house, my fever continued to take all my strength.

Since that time, someone came to stay here for three days. I couldn't eat anything but I drank water and Coca Cola. My legs are very swollen as well so a family member asked a doctor to come and he gave me shots of penicillin for which I paid 30 shillings. Now my leg is better but I have not been able to walk. Fr Matte has been here and seen my illness.

Your friend, Aniceti Kietereza

---

4 APRIL 1975 FR MATTE TO LARSON

Dear Miss Larson.

I hope all is well with you. We had no rain and then we got some but it did not rain again for some time; our poor people will not get any rice, little cotton, so hardly any revenue when prices go up so steadily.

Our friend Aniceti whom I saw after Easter is not too well; his legs are swollen. He spends all his time in bed. He is much worried; I could not help him much as I have no answer from you about my letter to you in February. I was inquiring then – what is your program towards helping Aniceti financially; how much per month, or every second month??? Then I would take care of him accordingly.

On your part, to save expenses, trouble and the rest, you would just credit me in Montreal as you have done before every three, four or six months. If at all possible I would very much appreciate answers to these proposals that Aniceti and get help regularly.

Everything is going well here, we are just wondering about the rain; otherwise it will be too late; luckily they have better rains on other parts of the country; there is no question of famine on this island, but then no money at all to buy some necessities like matches, kerosene for lamps, soap, meat, fish, salt, some cooking oil, clothes.

My best wises, union in prayers, yours in Christ. Charles Matte Nansio

---

21 JUNE 1975 KITEREZA TO HARTWIG URGENT!

Dear Dr. G. J. Hartwig,

I remember that it is eight months since I have heard from you. I also remember that I wrote you 31 October '74 thanking you for your gift of $35 which was brought to me by the hand of Fr van der Wee at the time we were being moved by the government to a new place.

I know you and Mama Hartwig have a great deal of work. Now, I am asking if you have any news of publishing my book, Myombekere. Where is it these days?! Please answer me soon about the English translation also.

On 17 June 1975, I welcomed guests from the Tanzanian government here at my house in Kagunguli Centre – they came from Dar es Salaam. They told me that they have seen my Swahili translation which came from the Ford Foundation in Nairobi brought there by John Allen. The representatives from Tanzania came from the Literature Department at the University of Dar es Salaam. They said they were very happy to receive a copy and want to publish it soon. They would like to see the original translation but when they inquired at Nairobi, they were told John Allen went to Europe. So they came to my home.

They asked that I write Mr. Allen or Dr. Hartwig so that they can proceed quickly. These guests from Dar es Salaam came in two cars. If you, Dr. G. Hartwig, have the original handwritten manuscript of Part 1 and Part II, please send it to Fr Nicola at Murutunguru Parish. Please send it quickly.

Rheumatism continues to bother me morning to night!! Your friend, Aniceti Kitereza

---

28 JUNE 1975 KITEREZA TO LARSON

Dear Miss Emilie,

Since I sent a letter of 3 May '75 thanking you for the $40 you sent to Fr Matte until today I have heard no news of you and how you are as well as David. Perhaps the letter was lost?

Today I don't have much to say but I am hopeful that my book Myombekere and Bugonoka will be published here in Tanzania in Kiswahili. On June 17, 1975, two guests from Dar es Salaam came to ask about the manuscript I wrote in Kikerebe and then Kiswahili. They have seen the translation from John Allen which they received from Miss Fisher of Ford Foundation in Nairobi. The guests were from the Literature Department of Dar es Salaam. They wanted to see Mr. Allen in Nairobi but he is now in Europe and so they need the hand written manuscript. Please, could you contact Dr. Gerald Jerry Hartwig about this and have him send it to Murutunguru for Aniceti Kitereza of Kagunguli Parish P.O. Box 16, Nansio Ukerewe Island.

My wife Anna greets you and David and your family! Your friend, Aniceti Kitereza

---

30 June 1975 Fr Matte to Larson

Dear Miss Larson,

Many thanks for your two letters of June 1st and June 18th. Yes, I had good holidays on the Indian Ocean; rainy season but still enough sun; anyway I did not go for the sun, we have more than we want here. I was with other WF, friends from Nairobi and Mombasa. A real good break with good seafood.

You sent something late May and again on June 14th though you did not mention the amount of late May. I suppose it was fifty dollars; anyway I'll hear about it from Montreal; I will see Aniceti today and bring him your two gifts. No problem, we can always arrange things, and I can do something for him also. Please do not bother about a small difference in value between American and Canadian dollars; I can easily manage that and good Aniceti will not be penalized for that.

Hope you are much better, that you can enjoy well deserved holidays in Minnesota; should be beautiful in July, plenty of lakes, I suppose, should not be far from Wisconsin?

Could you get for me two copies of Hartwig's HISTORY OF UKEREWE; you deduct the value from what you send later for Aniceti. I will refund Aniceti; the easiest way for me to pay for the books. Of course I have relatives and friends; I can afford it so I will not accept these books as gift, plus postage, of course.

No more rain; not until October if we are lucky; cotton is good; no rise; if enough moisture in the soil people will get sweet potatoes they planted some time ago.

Just saw Aniceti; his legs are a bit better; he is about 80 years old; his wife is very well; he was reading your letter with his Engish-German dictionary by his side; he is cheerful. A Tanzanian who teaches literature, also French, at the University of Dar es Salaam, gave him some hope that one of his books would be published; I do not know how serious these words are.

My best wishes, union in prayer, God bless you; have a beautiful summer. Fr Matte

---

2 July 1975 Kitereza to Larson

Your letter of 18 June '75 arrived the 30th of June with your checks of $50. Fr Matte brought it. My wife and I thank you very much. You continue to be such a generous person these many years remembering us in our poverty. We pray God to give you a long life and to bless you every day.

Dr. Hartwig wrote that he sent the manuscript of my book to Khartoum University in Sudan hoping that it could be published there. Really, Jerry has been a central support through all of this. The two of you have done great work.

Fr Matte has been here and seen my illness and my fear and doubts. I am still unable to walk, no appetite. My wife Anna suffers still with her heart. This year on our island of Ukerewe, we have had much rain during March so that many have good health, enough food with cash from their crops.

URGENT! I ask you please to contact Dr. Gerald Jerry Hartwig requesting that he send the original handwritten copy of my manuscript to Murutunguru, P.O Box 16, Nansio Ukerewe. This is important because the Manager of the Tanzania Publishing House requests this. So, please help and ask him to send it right away. Your friend, Aniceti Kitereza

---

7 July 1975 Hartwig to Kitereza

Dear Aniceti,

I have received your letter of June 21st and am delighted to learn that you have been visited by representatives from the University of Dar es Salaam.

I tried to mail the Swahili manuscript on July 3rd but ran into trouble with the postal rates. The way I had wrapped the manuscript it would have cost $24 (169/-) to mail. So I will wrap it again and send it air mail for Father Nicola on July 7th, the same day this is being mailed.

Although I have not written to you since October 1974, I have been informed about your activities. The letters you send to Emilie Larson are sent by her to Shoonie for translation!

There is no news about the English translation of Myombekere and Bugonoka. It was sent to Khartoum, Sudan, to see if the university press would be interested, but I fear that is not going to work either. Now I am unsure whether I should try another press or not. I have not heard from John Allen since last September. At the present time I do not have his address, but will write to him now and hope that the letter is forwarded to him.

I have been busy with my teaching and writing. The manuscript I wrote about the Kerebe should be off the press within the next two months. It was finished three years ago. Publishing is so very slow here in the U.S., just like it is in East Africa. A manuscript that Shoonie finished three years ago should also be published the end of this year. She wrote about people she met on Ukerewe. There is a chapter about you and Anna; also one on Bahitwa and one on Buyanza. I shall send you a copy when it is available.

I am pleased that the Swahili version of your manuscript may soon be published in Dar es Salaam. I am sure the English version will not be too much longer.

Greetings to Anna. We are all doing well and think of you and Anna often. Sincerely, Gerald Hartwig

---

7 JULY 1975 HARTWIG TO ALLEN

Dear Mr. Allen:

I have just learned from Aniceti that representatives from the University of Dar es Salaam visited him in June requesting the original Swahili version of his manuscript. I posted it via air mail to Father Nicola at Murutunguru Parish on July 7th. I trust it will arrive in good order.

I apologize for not keeping in touch with you during the past months. At this stage I'm not even sure what your address is so am sending two copies of this letter to the two addresses I have in hopes one of them will catch up with you.

Needless to say I'm pleased that someone at Dar has finally expressed an interest in Aniceti's work. How did you manage that?

I have absolutely nothing to report on the English translation ms. One lead has been pursued – University of Khartoum Press. It has unfortunately consumed nothing but time. Should I pursue Orbis Books (Maryknoll

Fathers)? Have you turned up any possibilities? I fear any publisher is going to request sizeable cuts in the ms. Because of this situation, I would prefer that you do the negotiating, which ever press is approached.

Before doing anything more, I intend to wait until I hear from you. If the worst develops, i.e., no one will undertake the English translation as it now exists, would you advice reducing the length for a paper bound edition or would you prefer a cloth bound version with an introduction from something like Duke University Press? I'm quite assured of being able to swing the latter option.

I shall await your reply. Sincerely,

Gerald Hartwig

Dear Hartwig,

Thank you for your letter of 7 July. I almost wrote to you when I first heard of the visit from representatives of the University (and/or the Tanzania Publishing house). I did not because I am resolved not to write until there is something concrete to report, and I will not succumb to optimism. Similarly I have not told Aniceti of all the efforts that I have made.

At the moment I think that we can do nothing at all. I have advised Aniceti that unless to do so means losing translation rights without a firm undertaking to publish the English edition within a reasonable time. Until we hear more we do not know what is the position regarding these rights. I have written to ask the TPH to let me know soon what is the position, so that I may call in my other current attempts if they have made a firm contract. I shall be surprised if I receive any answer at all. So I must wait to hear from Aniceti or Fr Nico.

Nevertheless, if you are sufficiently confident that you can persuade anyone to produce any form of English edition, you could write to TPH saying, I have a firm offer; do I go ahead or have you bought the translation rights? The original (Heinemann) plan was for a two volume paper back; but this was before I had dealt with Part II and realized how much cutting was desirable. My translation of Part II is in fact already quite considerably abbreviated. As between paper and cloth bound, I should prefer to accept your advise. The public at which we aim would primarily be the African Studies Depts of Universities and you know best what price they can stand. The publisher should himself propose the cuts and put them to Aniceti, who would, I am sure, agree. Neither you nor I can do any formal negotiation, because we have no legal position. I have made it perfectly clear that the English is as much the property of Aniceti as is the Swahili.

TPH received the Swahili ms from Miss Fisher of Ford Foundation. To what extent the Foundation is involved I have no idea; but it is possible that they are offering a subsidy. The speed at which these negotiations go is indicated by a letter from her to me last September saing that TPH promised a firm decision within three weeks.

Yours sincerely, John Allen

---

16 JULY 1975 ALLEN TO HARTWIG

Dear Hartwig,

In my letter of 10 July I grossly maligned the Tanzania Publishing House. I have a telegram from them reading, "Definitely publishing Kitereza in Kiswahili – English. Letter follows fortnight today – Bgoya."

I think that at last we can rest. I think that I can now congratulate you because it was your efforts that started the whole thing. Without you I should never have heard of Aniceti.

I have no idea how long it will take now before we actually see the book in print. I hope that we shall all live to see it.

Yours sincerely, John Allen

---

17 JULY 1975 FR MATTE TO LARSON

Dear Miss Larson,

Many thanks for your letter of October 4; I saw Aniceti yesterday, bringing along your gift; he was writing a letter to the Hartwigs, I think. He tries to take a walk around, to get a little exercise, with difficulty, using a stick, his legs always swollen; his wife was in bed, poor heart, I am afraid, also very weak. Aniceti received the missing pieces of his translation; he's very pleased.

Union in prayers, best wishes. Aniceti will certainly thank you personally. Fr Matte

---

18 JULY 1975 HARTWIG TO ALLEN

Dear Mr. Allen,

I have waited a few days before responding to your letter of July 16th indicating that Kitereza is to be published in Swahili and English. For some reason skepticism remains, although you definitely exuded optimism. I only hope that you are right. This ms has been on my conscience for eight years, on your mind for, what, five years? And then there is Aniceti, this marks the thirtieth year since is was completed. Oh me. Apparently the Ford Foundation has stayed committed.

Your part in this saga has been monumental; well done!

Best wishes, Gerald Hartwig

---

29 JULY 1975

Dear Dr. G. J. Hartwig,

Your letter of 7 July '75 arrived on 17 July '75. You told me that you had to repackage the manuscript due to cost. Thank you for this. BUT, I have discovered that in Part 1 there are two chapters missing. Loo! My friend, Gerald Jerry, please check quickly because without these, the publishers will not have the complete manuscript. My wife sends greeting to your family. I will be happy to receive Shoonie's book! Your friend, Aniceti Kitereza

---

16 OCTOBER 1975 KITEREZA TO HARTWIG

Dear G. J. Hartwig,

Your letter of September '75 arrived with a big package. Mr. Hartwig and Mama Shoonie, you have no worries now. All the chapters are there. I thank you so very much for finding them. For many years and since 13 February 1945 when I wrote first with the White Fathers and since you, Dr. Gerald Jerry Hartwig came to the island of Ukerewe for your research, you have helped me these many years – May God give you many years!

You said that you included an article recently published but it wasn't in the packet. Please send it!

Thank you for telling me about your children – the youngest is 5, Kari is 12, Karl is 14 and Christopher is 16. Loo! You are a young man with great strength! My wife sends greetings to all in your home. Greetings to all. Aniceti Kitereza

---

15 NOVEMBER 1975 LARSON TO WHITE FATHERS GENTLEMEN:

Enclosed is a bank money order for $150. May I, please, ask you to credit to the account of Father Jean-Charles Matte for Mr. and Mrs. Kitereza of Ukerewe Island, Tanzania?

My deepest appreciation for your help in making my contribution to these dear people possible.

Sincerely,

(Miss) Emilie G. Larson

Your letter of 15 November '75 arrived the 26th of November and Fr Matte brought us the money you sent for three months of October, November and December. My wife, Anna Katura, and I thank you so very much for your continuing generosity to us poor people. My wife suffers greatly from heart troubles!

My manuscript is going to be in two languages: Kiswahili and English. When I know more I will tell you and Dr. G. J. Hartwig. I am so happy. Please help us get copies. And I'd like a copy of Mrs. Shoonie's books. Loo! I will be so happy to read her book!
Wonderful!!

Our health continues to be difficult. Please greet your family. My wife sends Christmas and New Year greetings for 1976! Your friend, Aniceti Kitereza

---

4 DECEMBER 1975 KITEREZA TO HARTWIG

Dear G. J. Hartwig,

I can't remember well which day or which month that I received all the chapters of MYOMBEKERE. But you didn't answer my questions in my last letter. Perhaps you didn't receive it. I have news from Miss Emilie that your book will be published in January 1976! Please, my friend, send me a copy! Miss Emilie also told me that Mrs. Shoonie finished her book. Mama Shoonie, please send me one copy.

There are two young men here on Ukerewe who would like to study at your University in Carolina. Please answer me if there is room.

My book is near completion. I send you Christmas greetings – also from my wife Anna – and for the New Year 1976. Our health is not good. We pray for a good death.

Your friend, Aniceti Kitereza and Anna Katura

1976

There are only three letters exchanged during this year, testifying to the seven years of patient and enduring friendships.

---

24 June 1976 Hartwig to Kitereza

Dear Aniceti:

Finally, I have good news to report. My book about the Kerebe has at last been published. I am sending a copy to you in a separate envelope – by air- mail. It should arrive about the same time that this letter does. Enjoy reading it. I deeply regret that it was not ready sooner so that Buyanza could have seen it. His information was so very important to me. I think Emilie Larson is getting copies of the book for the priests, but it will be about six more weeks before they will receive any.

Do you have any news about your book from Tanzania Publishing House?

In a few weeks, July 19, Karl and I are going to Khartoum where I will start to study the Shilluk; they live on the Nile River about 350 miles south of Khartoum. We will stay only six weeks so it will be a short visit. Unfortunately we won't be able to visit Tanzania. It will be the first time for me to visit Africa since I left Tanzania in 1969.

Please give my greetings to Anna. Shoonie also sends her greetings to both of you. Sincerely,

Gerald W. Hartwig

20 July 1976 Kitereza to Hartwig

Dear Dr. G. W. Hartwig,

Your letter of 24 June '76 along with your book – The Kerebe and Long-Distance Trade, 1800 – 1895 – arrived safely July 6,

First, I want to thank you for sending me your book with the names of so many from this island of Ukerewe and so many of my family. Second, I see you have written to me by hand in the book and really, you have given me a great honor before so many. Also you write how I assisted you in the writing of this book. Very good!

Also I want to thank you and your wife for your gifts of two blankets. You have not forgotten us since you were here in 1969. Really, these blankets have been on our bed every night. Until now, Miss Emilie Larson helps us so very much. In a letter she wrote, "The Hartwigs and I have you very much in our thoughts at all times." We pray for your health and long life and blessings in your work every day. Amen!

I am starting to read your book Mr. Jerry and it brings me great joy. You wrote that you wished that my relative Buyanza could have seen it before he died. Could you tell me the cost of your book in shillings? I have not heard anything about my book from Tanzania Publishing House.

You are going to Khartoum to study the Shilluk near the Nile. Who are the Shilluk? And what are their specialties? I looked them up in my dictionary but I found nothing. Please help me understand!

We wish you could return to Tanzania! My wife and I send greetings to you, Mrs. Shoonie and the family. P.S. Dr. Gerald W. Hartwig – I've forgotten how long ago I asked you about two young men who wish to study at your university. Please tell me your answer – if there is room or not. Your friend, Mzee Aniceti Kitereza

26 July '76 Kitereza to Larson

Dear Miss E. Larson,

I understand that when Mama Shoonie translates my letters, you want to know more about my wife Anna Katura's health. She continues to suffer with coughing and can't get well. The doctors say that maybe it's an infection of some kind. Really, Miss Larson, we used to have doctors come to our home but now those old doctors are dead and that's two years ago. Loo!!

The government doctors, at the hospital, do not like to give good medicine to old people. They say it is useless to give them medicine for they have a short life; the young people will have a long life. OOH!

When my wife Anna Katura could not stop coughing, I sent her to Nansio to see a doctor and he took an X-ray but he couldn't see anything. He thinks the problem is in her lungs. Please, Miss Emilie, we don't know the name of a medicine to give Anna. Could you ask a doctor for a name? I could talk with Fr van der Wee and he could buy the medicine with some of the money you have sent me.

My generous friend, we are so very grateful to you for your kindness these many years. Every day we pray that God will continue to bless you. Mr. and Mrs. A. Kitereza

---

4 September 1976 Kitereza to Shoonie (written in English)

Mrs. Shoonie.

Your letter of 11th August '76 is arrives me safely on Wednesday 25th August '76. Oh! Mrs. Shoonie I am very rejoiced to receive again your best letters from many years ago. I saw that in this letter you have two languages written; the first is Swahili and the second is English.

Now let me try also reply you, but I will make use of my few words of my broken English. Doubtless, I think, you will laugh over my mistakes!

It is true as you have said that if I get your letter, I will quite wonder indeed. So Anna my wife and I, we are very cheerful in our small and narrow slope at Kagunguli village – Plot – House No. 72.

You said in your letter you are so old-person and this is the reason which does you the Swahili language forget? Are you eldest than your husband Jerry who born 1935? I think you are of same age or inferior. But I don't your age please let me know! Miss Emilie Larson every time she writs me that the Swahili letters from me she sends it to you per Air Mail to be translated for her! Thank you very much Mrs. Shoonie for your helpful!

This is the fifth paragraph in which I want to end my broken English. Also I begin to ask you for pardon because I have written badly a lot of many words but meaningless like the songster bird named "Parrot".

I think that your husband and Karl both are at home. Because The Hartwig has said they will stay only six weeks on Khartoum! Is it true or wrong? Give my greetings to Gerald W. Hartwig and his son Karl!

(continues in Swahili)

I am answering your letter with a few words in Kiswahili. My wife Anna Katura has returned home from the hospital in Nansio. Now we stay together in our house.

I understand that your husband and Karl went to Khartoum to study the Shilluk – similar to the study of the Bakerebe.

Really, Mama Shoonie, you are doing a lot of work teaching 25 students how to play the piano. At your church in Durham, North Carolina, you have a program using songs, dance, folk tales from Africa and America. You told me that I would enjoy it, and I would, really! You tell me that many who see this learn from the skill and ability of the young ones. You also tell me that you use our folk tale, "The monkey and the lizard" or Enkwambu and Enkende!

You also told me that your Mama is the same age as me, born in 1896 – 80 years old! Kurt is now six, busy with many things and happy. Kari is growing taller and Kristopher has just had his 17th birthday. Asante Mrs. Shoonie for sending me all this news. I hope that soon I will hear news of my book! My wife and I greet you and all your family. Your friend, Mzee Aniceti Kitereza

1977

Ten letters are written during this year. They are all blue aerograms, sent from Kitereza to Larson or Hartwig. By now, the format of Kitereza's letters is clear: date letter received, previous letters not answered, recounting news in letter, update on health. These excerpted letters will only include new information.

Miss Larson.

Your letter of 5 December 76, I received on 23 December 76, but I was surprised because I wrote letters to you thanking you for your gifts of three months: June, July and August and also I asked the price of Gerald W. Hartwig's book about the history of the Kerebe – but loo! – you didn't answer me. And, I haven't had an answer about the price from Mrs. Shoonie. I am thinking the letters are lost in the post? Or?

I am remembering your time here on Ukerewe Island when you passed through the Serengeti and saw many animals and since then you have helped us poor people. I read that Fr Matte visited you and you drank coffee together and you talked about Mrs. Shoonie's research about the music on our island. And also Mrs Samkange came to visit. And you talked with her about my work.

My wife and I pray that you have a long and good life.

I wonder if Dr. Jerry has returned from his trip to Khartoum?

I was sorry to read that your throat was so bad you couldn't sing in church but your doctor said you will get better. Your long letter of 5 December

76 told me many things. I couldn't answer each paragraph because of my lumbago as I can't sit long or stay in bed long. My wife Anna Katura greets you! Aniceti Kitereza

---

26 FEBRUARY 1977 KITEREZA TO LARSON

Dear Miss Larson,

My generous friend of many years, you wrote me a letter on 5 December 1976 and I replied quickly on 4 January 1977, but until today, I haven't heard from you. I know that Mama Shoonie translates them and it takes time and that you have much work to do.

Once again, I am writing you to know the price of Gerad W. Hartwig's book – THE ART OF SURVIVAL as there are many young people who wish to buy it but we need to know the price in shillings.

On 14 February '77, I received a letter from Fr Matte in Canada to tell me that he will return to Tanzania the month of March '77 but he will work in Dar es Salaam. He will come to Ukerewe and visit me here in Kagunguli. We pray God to give him health and us as well so we might see one another face to face. That will be joyous!

On 23 February '77, Fr van der Wee brought your gift for January '77. You continue to be our generous friend and we thank you very much. We pray God's blessing upon your work and all you do every day and that you have a long life until you are with God in heaven. Amin!

Please greet your Aunts, David and his family. My wife, Anna Katura sends many greetings. She continues to suffer with heart disease. Your friend, Aniceti Kitereza

---

17 MARCH 1977 FR VAN DER WEE TO LARSON

Dear Miss Emilie.

You may have noticed, I am not very fervent in answering letters. Thanks for your letter already from months ago. Everything is OK here. We have had a nice Easter, I hope you have the same. Fr Matte was here for some days to see some of his friends and pick his luggage. He is now in Dar es Salaam. He visited Aniceti Kitereza. They are all right.

I just go on paying him on monthly visits as I used to do. Since a couple of weeks we have got rains every day. It may be good for rice, but for cotton is it becoming too much. Let us hope for the best. I looked as if we were getting a good harvest, but now...

It is funny that the books of the Hartwigs, although it is a month ago that you wrote me have not arrived. The mail? Perhaps you could check it. Thanks.

Best wishes – Yours in Christ Fr van der Wee

---

17 April Kitereza to Larson

22 April 1977 Kitereza to Hartwig

Dear Dr. Gerald J. W. Hartwig,

Your letter of 1 April 1977 arrived on Monday the 20th of April. I was greatly surprised to receive it because it has been such a long time. I remember that you went to Khartoum for research and that your son went with you.

I know you have news of me because your wife Shoonie translates Miss Emilie's letters. We still wait for information regarding the price of your book.

Fr Matte visited us here in our home on 28 March '77. He will now live in Dar es Salaam. Perhaps he will be able to go the Tanzania Publishing House to hear about my book.

I am very happy to hear that your family is well. Here, our health is not good from morning to night.

P.S. Rheumatism along with Lumbago is very troublesome. When you get this letter, please answer quickly. Shoonie's book – is it finished yet? Your friend, Mzee Aniceti Kitereza

---

22 April 1977 Kitereza to Hartwig

…Fr Matte came to my home on the morning of 23 March '77. He is now working in Dar es Salaam – a long way away. Perhaps he will be able to visit The Tanzanian Publishing House.

---

9 May 1977 Kitereza to Larson

News from here on Ukerewe this year of 1977 is about rain since January until now, this month of May. Many houses have fallen because of floods. We are very afraid that our house will also collapse because it is on a 'slope'. There are many deaths.

3 JULY 1977 KITEREZA TO LARSON

Fr Matte wrote me from Dar es Salaam to say that the head of Tanzania Publishing House has my manuscript but there is much to do in his office. But he will continue to wait for what the head says.

18 AUGUST 1977 KITEREZA TO LARSON

On 11 August 1977, Fr van der Wee of Murutunguru Parish brought me news in a telegram saying that the second child of Shoonie and Jerry Hartwig – Karl, died in a motor- car accident. We have been so very sad. With the congregation and family of our Karl, we pray that God gives him great joy forever in heaven. Amin.

Your friend, Aniceti Kitereza

23 AUGUST 1977 KITEREZA TO LARSON

I have become an invalid with my rheumatism. I asked the Fathers to find me a tricycle but as yet they have not come with one.

17 NOVEMBER 1977 KITEREZA TO LARSON

I understand that Mr. Hartwig and his wife Shoonie gave you copies to send me of the church service for their son Karl. OO! We were overwhelmed with sadness to read it and to hear of the many family members who came. And this is also for Anna and me, we are so very sad because we knew him in 1968 when they were here for research. He was a kindly, loving child and we pray God to hold him well.

1978

Excerpts from nine letters continue as before.

About the tricycle: I gave Fr John Harding from the Catholic Church 2,350 Tshillings to buy it in Dar es Salaam. I waited a long time – seven months – before it arrived on 23 January '78 at 11:00 p.m. I tried to get on it but they sent the wrong size and without the handlebar! Loo!! I asked bicycle repairmen here to return it and request refund of the money. It is useless!! I don't know what they will say.

Bad news: On 6 January 78, Fr van der Wee of Murutunguru Parish became very ill. He was taken to the Sengerema Hospital but they couldn't help him. I just heard this very day that he will be taken to Europe in an airplane. I have so many troubles!

---

13 FEBRUARY 1978 KITEREZA TO LARSON

News of Fr van der Wee: He is now in Holland at a hospital where the doctors performed an operation. Because Fr van der Wee was your contact here, now it is important to write Fr Charles Matte in Dar es Salaam or perhaps he can ask someone here to be my agent.

---

12 APRIL 1978

On 8 April 1978, I was visited by Fr William Settles of Murutunguru parish. He is new and takes on the position of Fr van der Wee who is recovering from his operation in Holland.

Tell Mr. Jerry that I received four copies of the booklet remembering his son Karl. I will write him.

On 29 March 1978, I received a copy of my book: MYOMBEKERE. Now I must read it carefully for any errors. This is a lot of work – to be sure that the Kikerebe to Kiswahili translation is correct. They say that they hope to begin the English translation in 1978. Fr Matte is helping a lot as he is in Dar es Salaam and goes to the Tanzania Publishing House.

---

13 APRIL 1978 KITEREZA TO HARTWIGS:

Dear Mr. and Mrs. Hartwig:

On 31 March, I received a packet including four copies of A VIEW OF LIFE along with a letter. Oh my friends, I am filled with sorrow to know of Karl Walter Hartwig's death! Since the month of August 1977 until now you know overwhelming grief, my friends. I just have no more words to say for fear it will add to your sorrow. Know that here in my house, we continue to pray for our Karl Walter Hartwig.

News of my book MYOMBEKERE. I received a copy of Part I on 29 March 1978 and have begun editing for mistakes. The TANZANIA PUBLISHING HOUSE says they hope to complete it by September 1978! And then Part II will be ready in 1979!

---

6 MAY 1978 FR MATTE TO LARSON

I have already written that Mr. Aniceti gets his money for April; he has very good news; work is going on on his book; as I understand he has received an advance copy of his book from the publishers; some corrections still to be made; kiswahili is the medium; I do hope that they do not use too modern, too difficult kiswahili that very few people can easily and enjoy reading it. They create new words all the time.

JULY 6 1978 FR MATTE TO LARSON

I have just written to Ukerewe; Aniceti will get his due; I know he could not get too nervous about it, he very well knows that it is always coming. No news yet about the publication of his book.

---

19 AUGUST 1978 KITEREZA TO LARSON

I have been very sick with a high fever and hiccups that made my heart almost stop. After the doctor gave me medicine, my senses returned, but I stayed at the hospital at Kagunguli Centre. The doctors gave me food like porridge and sweet potatoes and milk. It was very expensive. My wife, Anna Katura had relatives with her but it cost more than 540 shillings to feed them for a month. I give thanks to God that I have lived to this day and I am able to give you this news of my illness.

11 October 1978 Kitereza to Larson

On 29 September – 78, Fr Charles Matte came here in the morning with his three sisters. Oh! My wife and I were very happy to have guests although they were in a great hurry. They brought two bottles of soda water! With my wife Anna Katura and me A.K. this was a wonder.

Father Matte brought me your gift my generous friend. It is now ten years since you came here with Hartwig and Shoonie and their family – two boys and one girl. Yes I have recovered from the fever but I am completely unable to move my legs. They hurt me a great deal I pray God for a good death.

On 29 September '78, when Fr Matte came here, he asked me, "Where is the 'Cripple Tricycle?" I told him that it is in the house of the Padres. I thought he would return it to Dar es Salaam but the tricycle is with a catechist in the Kagunguli parish. We thank you for everything and ask God to bless you!

23 November 1978 Matte to Larson

We saw Aniceti; very pleased to meet my sisters; not worse but no improvement either; he had bought a tricycle with pedals but he could not use it: too tall, too heavy, no room for his legs; we managed to collect money to buy it back from him and give the tricycle to a polio victim who is enjoying it very much.

I have written to Van der Wee today; he will handle your gift to Aniceti himself; he has still much pain in his legs and back, but I heard lately that things were improving. They are isolated now on the island, the boat Mwanza-Nansio is out of order for months to come, also the ferry between the island and the mainland.

1979

The first two of five letters from Kitereza to Larson recount news of health, the tricycle and East Africa.

---

4 August 1979 Kitereza to Larson

I have news that John Allen died on 6 April 1979 at his home in Oxford. 28 October 1979

I received a letter from Winifrida, wife of John Allen to tell me of his death. We knew him very well and together we worked on the translation of my book –MYOMBEKERE.

---

24 December 1979

BAD NEWS: Here in my house, my wife Anna-Katura is very very ill. They took her to Kagunguli hopital. She can hardly breathe. Her heart beats so fast that she doesn't know anything. I am so very sad. I do not know if she is able to recover.

Please send this news to Gerald Jerry Hartwig and his wife Shoonie.

1980

There are thirteen letters sent by Kitereza and Fr Matte to Larson and one to Hartwig.

---

28 FEBRUARY 1980 KITEREZA TO LARSON NEWS: MY WIFE,

Anna-Katura has left this world. She left me here all alone. On 7 February she died after three months of illness. I am late in writing but I couldn't because of my deep sorrow.

---

28 FEBRUARY 1980

Dear Gerald W Jerry Hartwig and Shoonie.

My dear friends, I have great sadness to tell you as my beloved wife, Anna-Katura has died. On 7 February 1980 she left this world at 12 noon after three months of illness, November, December, January. Oh! I am left here all alone in my poverty and illness. I am late to write you my friends because of my sorrow. Please let us all pray to God that Anna-Katura has a good place in heaven. Amin

---

27 MARCH 1980 MATTE TO LARSON

Dear Miss Larson,

A short note to let you know that Maria Katura, wife of Aniceti Ketereza died peacefully on February 7th. She had been in hospital; went home for about 4 weeks then died at home. Fr. v. d. Wee says she had become very thin, very weak; no pain, thank God.

You know they were a childless couple; very hard for him to have been faithful to his faith and to his wife; they certainly loved each other very much.

Certainly a great blow for him when due to his sickness he feels more or less unable to take care of himself; I am afraid he has very few relatives.

He will feel so lonesome; she was such a nice, quiet, kind person.

Let us pray for her, she was a really saintly person and pray to her that from Heaven she take proper care of her husband Aniceti. If I get more news I will let you know.

In Christ, Fr Matte

---

11 APRIL 1980 MATTE TO LARSON

I was on the island for 3 days; I paid a visit to Aniceti on March 17th; he has a good woman, a relative, to take care of him; he feels very lonesome, actually, aside from his book, not much interest left for him; he repeated: it will be my turn soon; with his deep faith, he is ready to go to his Father in heaven.

---

26 JUNE 1980 KITEREZA TO HARTWIGS (WRITTEN IN ENGLISH)

Dear, Dear! Both Friends. Mrs and Mr. Gerald Jerry Hartwig, as I received your best letter of 4 May '80 so I have seen and think this letter is the words of condolence of the death of my very beloved wife Anna Katura. Oh and now in this time I am wifeless and alone in my Sloping House here in Kagunguli Centre.

What can I do by the might of God" except to give honour and praise him self only! I know exactly that the world is full of troubles. However today I will make an effort to force out my shame; which makes me tremble as I have fever! Wonderful!!

Please forgive my broken English which I am going for to write it now to answer your best letter which you have send me on 9th May 1980. Yes. Dear Mrs and Mr Gerald Jerry Hartwig, I remember the day you came to my home with your children, as I was a dweller in my village Nakisilira. And in time of your work of historical research in the period of 1968-69.

Thank you very much Dear Mrs and Mr Gerald Jerry Hartwig to give me unchangeable constant and reminiscent of mine and Anna's faithful devotion to one another over many years from our youth to old age. I have understood that now in Anna's death, I share the bond of love of our Lord. And this is truly Anna have given me a gift of living that I shall always remember!

I have seen here a book written by Mrs. Shoonie, but the name of this book is THE BOOK AND THE DRUM. Oh, I was very astonished to see my big-picture inside of the Book; and next I saw my life and Bahitwa's just so the life of my eldest brother Bernardino Buyanza! Oh! I was very glad to see those things! So I remember that formerly I heard the information from Miss Emilie Larson that Mrs Shoonie had written a Book against myself! Oh! Dear Shoonie, I think that you have forgotten to send me a copy. Please send me copies of THE BOOK AND THE DRUM. My relatives and many people of Bukerebe want more to get this Book! Mrs Shoonie Gerald Jerry Hartwig can you please send me some copies?

Yes Dear, I agree that you know well my days and nights, I have sorrow in my loneliness! True, may the Almighty God continue to surround me with his love and His peace. Because, God, is alone LOVE!

---

10 NOVEMBER 1980 MATTE TO LARSON

So sorry about the news: the death of Jerry Hartwig; so young, so gifted and still so much to do; I found the Rector's very comforting words with such a solid basis as the Bible. I will remember him in my Mass and Prayers.

<h1 style="text-align:center">1981</h1>

I was so very sad to read of Jerry's death. You said he died on a Sunday, the 19th of October, sitting in a chair near his daughter and he had heart sickness!! But he died suddenly. I profess this from my heart: All men on this earth will one day die. Those left behind, the living, we pray to the Spirit of God to receive them a long life in Heaven!

Amin

Also, I know that Jerry's wife, Shoonie, suffers great sorrow. She is left behind, like me. Truly, she has had great troubles. Indeed, it is the way of this world. I will be writing her condolence.

Dear Miss Larsen,

Fr van der Wee told me that he had written to you the sad news; the death of our friend Aniceti.

A gifted person for sure; spiritually and intellectually; he was a catechist for many years, working with the parish priest Fr Simard many years, dictionaries; French- Kikerewe and Kikerewe French; also translation of the New Testament in Kikerewe which was later printed; he was my Kikerewe teacher when I was there in 1944, unfortunately for a few months only; he was always kind, helpful, witty, always smiling, a deep faith, being faithful to his marriage though he had no children, intelligent, knew good German, yes, an outstanding man, a good influence on all who had the opportunity to know him.

Having no children, you gave him something of very much value, by your help; security when old and sick, unable to look after himself. Miss Larsen, the best; you were an 'ange' for Aniceti, you certainly chose a most deserving fellow; may God give you the hundredfold.

So ends this remarkable exchange of more than two hundred letters. Over these eleven years, the correspondents' primary focus has been to publish Kitereza's novel. However, what we learn about his lived Ukerewe world as well as those writing reveals the very personal kinship that developed between all. It is a prelude to the continuing publishing epic.

Two weeks after Kitereza's death, two copies of *Myombekere* arrived in the Nansio post office. Although he had received the copy edition for editing, he never held the final Kiswahili publication.

In 1985, a book review entitled, "An Extraordinary Novel Out of Africa," appeared in *Development Dialogue*, authored by M. M. Mulokozi, writes:

> Throughout his many years, Kitereza has had more than his rightful share of life's tragedies. In many ways, the tragic streak of his life is paralleled in the lives of his major characters, Bwana Myombekere and his wife, Bibi Bugonoka. They, like Kitereza, are obsessed by a desire for offspring.
>
> Thus begins the story of the adventures of this unhappy Kerebe family who is supposed to have lived sometime in the seventeenth or eighteenth century. It revolves around the twin poles of production and reproduction, creation and procreation. Through production, within the framework of his clan, his village, his kingdom, and the accompanying traditions, beliefs, customs and taboos, Kerebe man produces wealth in order to build his *eka* (or household) and hence realize his humanity and his manhood. This he can achieve by interacting and cooperating with his fellow humans, obeying the common law, and not daring to go beyond the limits sanctioned by society in whatever he does.
>
> The purpose of labour is to build the *eka*, the purpose of marriage is to consolidate that *eka* by supplying it with offspring who will both protect and perpetuate the *eka* and, through the *eka*, the clan and, ultimately, the species. Hence the need for interaction and exchange, both human and material, between different *eka*, different clans.
>
> And this is where the central problem of this story lies, for Myombekere and Bugonoka fail to have children. Without children, what basis is there for him and Bugonoka to remain united in marriage? Can love alone sustain marriage in a society where offspring come before everything else, where barrenness is a social stigma? More seriously, can Myombekere and Bugonoka build their *eka* without offspring? How, and what for? Can life have any meaning without children?

This novel is, in short, a mine of ethnographical, historical and scientific information about pre-colonial Bakerebe and its people. Yet it is not history, nor is it, strictly speaking, a historical novel. All the characters are imaginary, all the incidents fictitious. There is no mention of the reigning kings nor any appraisal of their historically known actions. There is very little about the political feuds and upheavals that characterized the Kerebe Kingdom in the eighteenth and nineteenth centuries. All this is beyond Kitereza's intentions. His primary objective is to preserve the language, customs, practices and cultural traditions of the Bakerebe, seen from the point of view of the ordinary nineteenth century Kerebe, for the benefit of future generations. *Bwana Myombekere na Bibi Bugonoka na Ntulanalwo na Bulihwali* is primarily and deliberately a cultural novel.

This work remains a classic of Swahili literature. It is the longest Swahili novel ever published, the most racy, and the richest culturally. Without question, it establishes Kitereza as a leading Swahili – nay – African novelist, and the first and last of his kind.

Bwana Myombekere na Bibi Bugonoka is not only Kitereza's masterpiece, it is his *eka*. For without offspring he has, in the Kerebe view, no *eka*. His *eka* is this book, in which he placed all his talent and aspirations. It is his only child, and his only wealth (at the time of his death he was a very poor man living in a one room hut built for him by the Kagunguli Ujamaa villagers). His greatest desire, as he admitted to the present author, was to see his book in print before his death."

In 1985, the English translation of Kitereza's book was published by Mkuki na Nyota Publishers in Dar es Salaam, Tanzania. Dr. Gabriel Ruhumbika, an Mkerebe, translated *Myombekere* from its original Kikerebe text to English. In his introduction, he states:

"Kitereza's novel is significant for more than its content. It also adds to a new style of African literature, for Kitereza adopted an innovative storyteller style. Rather than merely transcribing African oral stories or imitating traditional African literature, Kitereza used the old art form to create a new kind of work. He narrated his story like a traditional African storyteller employing an array of oral-tradition conventions to create a work that depicts better-defined characters than conventional oral stories and seeks to explore in depth human and social experiences. It is this innovative style, which, more than anything else, makes his work both an important African contribution to world literature and a milestone in the growth of modern African literature.

Ruhumbika then quotes Hartwig:

> To seek and find and then share the secrets of life in a bygone era, to discover 'those things loved and those things despised' became his goal, enabling him to write a story of universal significance, because it concerns common people, those whose daily unglorified existence and beliefs must be respected because they are ours.

Since *Myombekere*'s English translation, it is now available in German and French. Kitereza's *eka* lives on, beyond the isolated shores of Ukerewe in Lake Victoria. It lives on, beyond its first language of Kikerebe. It lives on because his particular response to 'what should we teach our children?' is universal.

Aniceti Kitereza is the worlds' extraordinarily ordinary epic.